IMAGES OF WAR
MOTORCYLES AT WAR

RARE PHOTOGRAPHS FROM WARTIME ARCHIVES

GAVIN BIRCH

Pen & Sword
MILITARY

First published in Great Britain in 2006
Reprinted in 2007 by
PEN & SWORD MILITARY
an imprint of
Pen & Sword Books Ltd,
47 Church Street, Barnsley,
South Yorkshire.
S70 2AS

Copyright © Gavin Birch, 2006, 2007

ISBN 1-84415-408-4
ISBN 978-1-84415-408-1

A CIP catalogue record for this book is available
from the British Library

Printed and bound in Great Britain by CPI UK

Pen & Sword Books Ltd incorporates the imprints of
Pen & Sword Aviation, Pen & Sword Maritime,
Pen & Sword Military, Pen & Sword Select, Pen & Sword Military Classics,
Leo Cooper, Wharncliffe Local History

For a complete list of Pen & Sword titles please contact:
PEN & SWORD BOOKS LIMITED
47 Church Street, Barnsley, South Yorkshire, S70 2AS, England.
E-mail: enquiries@pen-and-sword.co.uk
Website: www.pen-and-sword.co.uk

Contents

WVS (Women's Voluntary Service) motorcyclist Meg Moorat is handed a message to deliver on her Triumph motorcycle, with civilian registration number FUL 166, in May 1941 outside the WVS Headquarters, London. One of the many civilian bikes 'impressed' for wartime service. (IWM HU90302)

Acknowledgements

Thanks to Brigadier Henry Wilson and the Pen & Sword Books Limited team, Mr Robert Coult of Hampshire – Prototype Welbike owner and mine of information, and all the restorers and riders worldwide with original wartime Motorcycles whose interest in this engaging aspect of Second World War history has made this book possible. I also thank the staff of the Photographic Archive of the Imperial War Museum, especially Elizabeth Selby, Sarah Martin, Claudia Condry for research guidance and Kirsten Matheis for coordinating workflow of the copying of these prints, and to Peter Hart for introducing the wealth of material held in the Sound Archives.

Sgt Norris of the AFPU (Army Film and Photographic Unit) captured this new safety device on 25 October 1944 designed by Sgt Wilson, Corps of Military Police, which consisted of a metal rod fitted to the front of his Ariel motorcycle. As the machine rode at wire stretched across the road by a retreating enemy the bar lifted the wire over the head of the rider allowing him to pass harmlessly. (IWM B11243)

A brief mention too of the ex Don-R (Army slang for a Despatch Rider, 'DR' originating during the First World War from phonetic sound enabling quick Morse coding, Don = D) who provided inspiration for this book. A veteran of the war through Northwest Europe he recounted tales of riding a 500cc BSA M20 through deserted French villages, evacuated of local populace, and frequently encountering the enemy. The memories returned of dodging under wire stretched across roads by retreating Axis forces – rigged to decapitate Allied motorcyclists, and of tucking his Sten gun down inside his Wellington boots having relentlessly practised quick-drawing and slamming the magazine home. All that after laying the bike down in controlled dismount. 'It wasn't like they show it in the films.'

Gavin Birch (c) 2006

Chapter One

Horseman to Horsepower

Military Motorcycles: The Origins

The British wartime 98cc Excelsior Welbike with Villiers Junior Deluxe horizontally mounted engine, the British paratrooper's folding scooter, was designed to fit in a 15 inch diameter D shaped drop container for Special Operations Executive (SOE) agents in the early war years. As the SOE agent descended by parachute into occupied territories the concept was that he or she was accompanied by the container dropped simultaneously delivering the Welbike. Once on the ground the agent would collapse their chute, construct the bike from its folded down form, bury parachute and drop container, and ride off on the bike to rendezvous with friendly contacts. The bike would be disposed of shortly after having provided the necessary getaway from the drop-zone. Designed and built by a pre-war ex road racer and motorcycle shop owner by the name of Mr Harry Lester, under the auspices of SOE's Lieutenant-Colonel J.R.V. Dolphin, the Welbike was born at an SOE design and research establishment known as 'The Frythe'. Lester was employed not only for his biking experience, but on the basis that he was an accomplished alloy welder (a skilled and difficult process) and was able to experiment with lighter weight materials competently in frame construction. The Frythe was located in Welwyn, UK, and hence many of the new weapon designs concocted there for secret agents gained the name 'Wel-*something*' and the mini-folding motorbike was no different in this respect to the agent's silenced Welrod Pistol, or Welman/Welsub mini submersible. This use of pre-war motorcycling expertise was a pattern that emerges often when considering the British approach to wartime motorcycle use. Stars of pre-war speedway and road racing were encouraged not only to test new machinery but to participate in the training of new recruits with the passing on of expert knowledge, and even to front recruitment drives. SOE rejected the finished product but the little machine was adopted by British Airborne Forces eager to expand their mid-war arsenal. The Welbike was carried ashore on 6 June 1944 during Operation OVERLORD and was flown into Arnhem later that summer for the September operation called MARKET GARDEN. Photographs of Welbikes taken in action are rare although prints of them used in

April 1944: Pre-Normandy Invasion exercises at Bulford Camp in Southern England show paratroopers unpacking Welbikes from specially designed D-shaped equipment containers which were dropped by air. Welbike has serial number C5154465. (IWM H37733)

training are included in this book. One German eyewitness record of their use at Arnhem features in the book 'The Dutch SS' (Armando & Sleutelaar, Bezige, 1978). Original Welbikes can be seen on display in several museums across the UK and Europe – particularly at the Hartenstein Hotel in Oosterbeek, Holland and at the Imperial War Museum, London. There are also a handful of examples in private hands in the UK, and Europe although the D-shaped drop containers they were designed to be air-dropped within are even rarer. Original Welbikes abound in the States too, where they were shipped after the war and sold as luxury children's toys by a well known department store. At least one prototype example survives in private hands also in the UK.

One only has to compare the little Welbike with the robust heavy duty 750cc German *Wehrmachtsgespann* BMW R75 and Zundapp KS750s with driven sidecars, some equipped with reverse gears, to quickly observe remarkable differences in design and intention. The German motorcycle combination was often armed with an MG34 and later more powerful MG42 machine gun, and designed with mainly standardised interchangeable parts. Frank V. Hurrell, a British NCO Artificer serving with a Recovery and Repair Section with 3rd Field Army Workshops, Royal Army Ordnance Corps in France in 1940 first came across the German combinations during the retreat to the French coast as it was motorcyclists who formed the frontline fighting arms for the Axis advance in 1940:

'We were told to head due north, just make for the coast because our 18 Pounders couldn't engage the enemy – the SS spearhead of the advance were using fast motorcycle combinations, a bike and armed sidecar, and people forget that the Germans made little use of infantry with their tanks in the early days.'

The motorcycle and sidecar became an offensive weapon during the Second World War but was utilised in roles from armed reconnaissance, to message delivery, recreational fun, to traffic control and display team workhorse by all the participants worldwide. This book considers the many diverse models, the feats of engineering, and sheer numbers of worldwide manufacturers involved in transporting the soldier on two wheels during the 1939 – 1945 war. It was an intention with this book to include some of the prototypes, standardised machines, and 'specials' built for racing and to provide a pictorial view of their use in combat theatres and on the home front demonstrating the range of two-wheeled machines of the British, Canadian, American and German Forces. To achieve this some of the caption information is less detailed than with other official images but a selection process has attempted to balance an interest for the current motorcyclist with that of the military historian from the range of source material consulted.

However no publication of this size can cover every model and therefore a selection of wartime photographs have been chosen to tell the story of the two wheeled war. The photographs included have mostly originated in the Photographic Archive of the Imperial War Museum – such an excellent research resource with a collection now totalling over ten million images of twentieth century conflict and the collection is growing every week! These photographs have their individual copyright administered by the museum, and anyone interested in using these or similar prints for publication should contact the archive. (photos@iwm.org.uk)

To begin our consideration of the procurement of motorcycles on all sides in the Second World War we must return to 1918 and the lessons learnt after the Great War when the change from horseman to horsepower was truly effected in Britain and America and to a lesser extent in Germany which was to continue its desire for equestrian transportation long after other countries mechanised.

During the Battle of Bazentin Ridge a German prisoner helps push this Royal Engineer Dispatch Rider's belt driven Triumph 3½ HP WD machine through the mud of Mametz Wood. Equine inspired saddlebags are secured over the fuel tank in this shot taken on 17 July, 1916 during The Somme Offensive. Some 30,000 Triumph motorcycles were supplied to the British Army during WWI, earning themselves the nickname of 'The Trusty'. Powered by a single cylinder four stroke power unit driving through a Sturmey-Archer three speed gearbox, and equipped with a kick starter it became very popular with British troops. (IWM Q3972)

The British Army rounded the year of 1918 out with a full complement of the weapons and equipment required to fight set-piece European warfare for the future. A victorious army, and confident, which was willing to review the lessons learnt over four years of arduous trench stalemate, and conflict in far off destinations. The

General Staff took a short pause, and then in 1919 began to piece together a form of doctrine which hoped to restore the notion of mobility into the battlefields of the future avoiding costly attritional stand-offs experienced throughout 1914-18. The looming task for the 1919 Army however was clearly not to fight a new large scale European war, but instead to rapidly set about Frontier protection and policing of Empire. These tasks placed a premium on mobility rather than the ability to create instant and massive firepower. That said, mobility through mechanisation was an idea very much still under experimentation during the Great War, and with peacetime, further exploration would continue.

In 1915 a regular division of the BEF fighting on the Western Front was only equipped with around eleven motor cars, four motor lorries, nineteen motorcycles and twenty-one motor ambulances. Although the internal combustion engine had

Exhausted motorcycle despatch riders rest on their Douglas 2³/₄ HP solo belt driven motorcycles at the roadside in Feuchy on 5 June, 1917. The missing front mudguard on the bike laying down has been replaced by an improvised leg shield as on the bike in the rear to provide some splash protection for both riders. Note the dents and missing steel from their helmets. The larger Douglas 4 HP bike was used when fitted in a sidecar-bike combination. (IWM Q5468)

been hailed as a wonder since 1884, it was still an unreliable wonder. Reliability could be found in the horse, proven, tested and battle hardened: the original go anywhere Mk I military vehicle. The motor car was incapable of travelling cross country, and delays with both supply of hand built spare parts, and the training of mechanics who knew how to repair the new motor vehicles provided additional doubts. Horse versus horsepower – the debate dragged on. The horse on the other hand appeared to be able to do everything demanded of it in the first years of the Great War. In 1914, months before the war started, the British Army was established for around 25,000 horses, and immediately after mobilisation this figure grew to 165,000. A year later and the demand had grown further to around 500,000 horses, 368,000 of which were on the Western Front. In more exotic climes 47,000 camels, 11,000 oxen and 6,800 donkeys were being put to use in the war effort. Along with the horses there were 82,000 mules on the Western Front which worked the more arduous tasks such as shell transportation to the guns in saddle bags. By the close of 1917 the number of equine animals on all fronts totalled near a million. The horse and mule were put to work in wide-ranging roles. Commanders used them as the fastest method to reach point B from A, and in an infantry battalion the Commanding Officer, all his company commanders and the adjutant had a horse to hand. The Field Artillery needed to get its guns where the infantry were quickly in order to support them, and this movement rarely adhered to metalled roads. Horses were the ideal tractor units for the guns and limbers. Each Brigade of Field Artillery had 108 horses, both to pull guns and haul ammunition wagons. If one studies official British film 'The Somme' from 1916 made during the battle one notes the mixing of mules and horses in gun teams. In this same pioneering early age of radio communication the despatch rider on horseback was far more likely to get a message to a number of drop off points quicker, and over greater distance than any radio message or telegraph – wires were often cut by enemy troops or by shelling. Lastly, there was the cavalry – such a proven force of times past, and that still experienced some lightning speed attacks during the Great War despite many publications that tell us they were an outmoded force. There were drawbacks however. Man-power requirement increased drastically with an expanded Veterinary Corps increasing from 508 all ranks in 1914 to 1,668 officers and 41,755 other ranks by 1918. Shipping was tied up in supply – not only for feed and other materials, but further afield in the purchase of, and return to the UK of suitable mounts which British breeders could not supply. Mounts were brought to the UK from Canada, the US and Africa. Training new animals, blacksmithing and leather working the saddles and bridles all required time not to mention the recuperation of the injured animals, and the nursing effort on a journey back to health. Skilled tradesmen were required to carry out the work, and they needed to be trained. One of the more

German despatch riders pose on a range of bikes used for message delivery in the German Army of the First World War. The photograph was taken in Palestine, 1918 and goggles appear to be the only specialist equipment provided to the rider. (IWM Q100333)

A similar Douglas 2¾ HP motorcycle to those featured in IWM Q 5468 this time being ridden in 1915 at Camp Cleopatra, in Egypt. Here a factory fitted front mudguard is visible, and a rear top box has been added along with the standard leather tool holdall to the rear mudguard structure. Motorcycles were being shipped out to all fronts during the 1914-18 war. Photo annotated on the rear: 'on my mo-bike!' (Author's own collection)

heartbreaking experiences for many of the troops was observing the injured animals, shelled or shocked, and bound together in the traces of ammunition wagons or gun limbers. The army patented its own 'humane killer' during this period, but the injured horses repeatedly crop up as a disturbing memory when one listens to interviews with veterans of the Great War. Records show that more animals died from respiratory illness than shellfire and yet the imagery endures.

With hindsight of course we can see that the writing was on the wall for the involvement of horses in warfare, but they were still heavily utilised by the German Army of the Second World War, despite it having the reputation as the mechanised originator of Blitzkrieg attack. In the civilian agricultural industry the horse was being replaced by the tractor, and new machinery was being implemented across the country that could be towed by track laying vehicles. Tanks had made their debut during the Somme offensive in September 1916 and the technology of war was advancing at a faster pace than ever before with the advent of the machine gun, landmine and flame thrower and tactics to match. Innovation stemmed from the extended period of stalemate with enemies facing each other over the expanse of No Man's Land and all the lessons to be found there. In 1919 the Army needed to look at newer methods of returning mobility to its troops, and one area, amongst many it was considering, was the implementation of the motorcycle on a much larger scale than had ever been envisaged during the fighting of 1914-1918. War production had provided profit and rapid innovation for many motorcycle manufacturers, and had ensured their existence and further development through the 1920s. AJS, BSA, Norton, Triumph and Douglas among others produced bikes for the British Army in the First World War. Douglas devoted its entire production runs between 1916 – 1918 to the Army producing variants of its Side-valve Twin of 1913 design (25,000). Triumph produced some 30,000 of its Model H 500cc variants, which also fared well in the post-war motorcycle boom of the 1920s when finished in civilian colours. With thousands of veterans returning home demanding cheap transport for daily commuting, and the army considering mechanisation issues it would not be long before the expanding motorcycle industry and the military would partner again during the inter-war years for further mutually beneficial experimentation.

Chapter Two

Interwar Experimentation

Senior British officers such as Sir Jock Burnett-Stuart, GOC-in-C Egypt realised that through the lessons of the 14-18 war the clues to preparedness and the winning of future conflict were to be found. He wrote in 1931:

'The days of linear extensions with each man separated by a stated interval are over. It's a matter of infiltration, of intelligent co-operation, and of taking immediate advantage of opportunities which the action of neighbouring parties might open up...'

(Burnett-Stuart, Training in Egypt, 1931)

The motorcycle it was then believed was the machinery that could facilitate this type of fast-moving, fluid co-operation amidst the general appreciation for a more mechanised force in Britain. The mechanisation process gathered pace through the early 1920s and between 1925 and 1939 received a concerted effort both in testing and securing the right type of machines and providing the best training for the men who would ride these motorcycles into action. This process was assisted not only by the British Army's conviction that motorcycles were essential for future combat, but by Britain's economic downturn in the 1930s. Civilian purchases began to drop away with the Depression and the future of many motorcycle manufacturing businesses was in doubt. Military contracts provided guaranteed income, and also a prestigious advertising by-line in the phrase 'As supplied to His Majesty's Armed Forces' and so the manufacturers actively pursued War Department Officials with their catalogues and impressive demonstrator models. Such contracts could mean the purchase of thousands of motorcycles, tentatively at least hundreds of models, so great import was placed upon meeting the WD requirements for a military motorcycle. To ensure the British army was getting what it was asking for, a tough testing programme was put into operation. Each new model of bike was sent to staff at the MWEE, (Mechanical Warfare Experimental Establishment) which changed name in 1934 to simply MEE (Mechanical Experimentation Establishment) and subjected to rigorous and exhaustive testing at tracks and workshops located at Cove, near Farnborough in the UK. Other locations were also used. The process instigated by these government bodies was aimed at providing a straightforward answer to the question of which models would be suitable for WD Service. The tests ranged over a 10,000 mile on and off-road assessment, where the bike would be stripped at various intervals for inspections on wear and tear, coupled with performance checks such as standing starts over quarter mile tracks, and cross-country abilities tested over a variety of surfaces including mountain, bog, river crossing, ditches and loose gravel surfaces. All test results were compiled into a single report per bike, and verdict provided. Included over the next pages are some of the many models sent by various British manufacturers for War Department testing in the hope of securing these lucrative and 'survival guaranteed' contracts between 1926 and the outbreak of war on 3 September 1939. Over a decade of investment of time, money, and thought went into this selection process. Bike and components were put through simulated 'war service' in efforts to expose the machines not capable of the job. It is remarkable and reassuring that such a process did take place to ensure that British troops received in *this* instance the very best and most suitable equipment the War Office was able to supply. Accepted for service were a range of 500cc models for the duration, some 350cc and even lighter 125cc. The smallest cubic capacity for an engine accepted into service was 98cc and largest was the heavier 1200cc imported from the US. As we shall observe, the British bikes performed very solidly throughout the war but in the decade before the 1939 declaration everyone manufacturing motorcycles in the UK was offering sample models for the MEE to test.

'Gentlemen – test those engines...'

One of the first machines tested in the quest for the perfect War Department motorcycle was this 1926 Triumph 494cc SV Single-Cylinder three wheeler which later spawned OEC models of similar design. The idea of three wheelers followed on from the testing and purchase of six-wheeled lorries for the Army of which the rear wheels on articulated bogies were chain driven with a linking belt which was thought to improve cross-country traction . The trend spread to motorcycle design. Tested at Aldershot it was found to handle well over rough terrain, especially when its rear wheel track was fitted creating a mini-halftrack. However its low ground clearance, weight and complex design went against it. Riders could hardly keep it upright cross-country. OEC were handed the test results and asked to improve upon this Triumph design. (IWM HU93252)

An MWEE photograph from 1929 of a modified Francis-Barnett Model 12 with increased engine capacity from the production 250cc to suggested military spec 350cc. This was achieved by enlarging the cylinder bores. Three of these types were bought for the 1929 seven manufacturer trials and when testing was completed late that year the machine did not make the grade. Being a two-stroke engine, it lacked cross country ability which appears to have been a war office criticism of all two-strokes throughout the testing process. Looking at the frame and components one notes its light construction in comparison with weightier bikes under test at the time. (IWM HU93259)

This smaller engined OEC 250cc 3-wheeler featured in the OEC catalogue of the period was referred to as a cross-country tractor, but photographed here in 1928 under test at MWEE wearing the WD census number C 19622 on its fuel tank. Both three wheelers have been fitted with spiked bi-pod leg stands to assist the test riders in keeping the bikes upright however these bikes were rejected. (IWM H93258)

With WD motorcycle census number C19621 this is a Triumph inspired OEC manufactured 350cc 3 wheel inline invention photographed under test at MWEE. Fitted with a Blackburn SV engine, it proved difficult to control during the testing process which continued until mid 1929, and weighing in at 354lb was considerably heavier than two wheeled samples under test. It was therefore rejected as the additional weight created by the articulating bogie supporting two rear wheels hardly enhanced cross-country ability. (IWM H93257)

One of the British manufacturers chasing major WD contracts between 1939-1945 was Sunbeam. Having originally supplied equipment in the First World War on a large scale they continued a relationship with the War Department submitting their 1936 Lion model for testing at Farnborough. Pictured here with a civilian number plate, the Sunbeam Lion was a 500cc SV Single Cylinder. Sturdy machine characteristics which drew upon the Norton 16H Model hoped to persuade the MWEE to recommend Sunbeam instead of Norton for a large order. However, Sunbeam was bought out by AMC who already produced their own successful military bike (the G3) and so the Sunbeam Lion was quietly dropped, the testing process never completed. (IWM HU93251 & IWM HU93250)

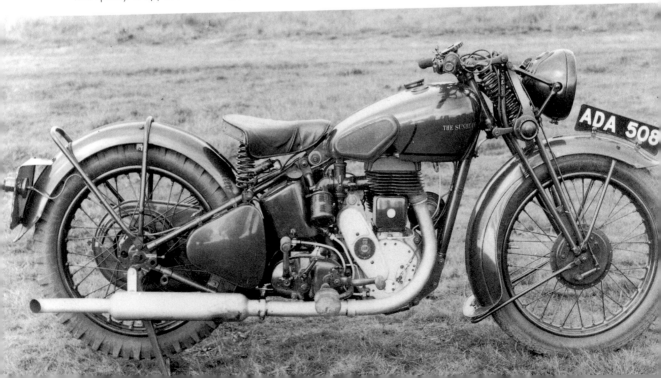

During a period in 1935 the War Office trialed a range of bikes produced by seven of the leading UK manufacturers. This is the Triumph 3/1 343cc SV Single-Cylinder model, one of those requested by the War Office. Triumph had an established relationship with the British Army and this model appeared promising. When trials began it was fitted with a hand-change gearbox, but after 2,415 miles it was converted to foot-change. The model under test suffered severely, with problems noted including stripped magneto driving wheels, and sheared armatures. The bike was unable to continue testing after 4,530 miles and was in fact dropped from the Triumph range due to company reorganisation simultaneously. MEE's final conclusion was that the performance of the machine had good cross-country ability, despite mechanical failings. (IWM HU93254 & HU93255)

The replacement model for the 1935 Triumph 3/1 was the Triumph Model 3S, 343cc, SV Single-Cylinder of 1936 which also went straight to MEE for military testing. The 3S featured a strengthened frame and new gearbox design, plus revised forks, fuel tank, wheels and other smaller parts. Testing revealed the Triumph 3S suffered from excessive cylinder wear in the engine, but again scored well in general reliability therefore being noted as suitable for War Office use – with some modification. (IWM HU93256)

In civilian paint scheme a Royal Enfield Model B, 250cc SV Single-Cylinder model of 1935 under test. The Model B was the only civilian model to be tested in 1935 alongside the other military trials, but mechanical weaknesses and poor endurance led to quick rejection – along with many minor faults the frame of the bike twisted during part of the 10,000 test process! The weak construction can be observed via the thin tube utilised on the frame. (IWM H93260)

A modified commercial model 1936 Rudge Whitworth 'Rapid' test model loaned to MEE, Farnborough for testing. However, like many other civilian bikes accepted for testing it was found only to be 'fair' after arduous 10,000 mile experimentation. Offered as a potential replacement for standard War Office motorcycles, it was, like so many others, not adopted. Some Rudge models did find their way into Army service in small numbers at the beginning of the war but there were no large contracts for this manufacturer. (IWM HU93249)

Ariel submitted a number of models for testing including the Ariel W/VA. Small orders were placed for this 497cc model by the War Office as it matched the standards set by the Norton 16H and BSA M20 in terms of power and strength which had been supplied since 1939. The W/VA was an altered version of the civilian design and was suited to second line duties including RAF and Women's Land Army use, but Ariel were keen to develop further models. Note the rocket fin exhaust pipe detail – also part of the detailed components' testing process. (IWM HU93233 & IWM HU93234)

The BSA War Office 498cc V Twin, converted to a foot gear change, as later BSA Twins all were, was produced between 1933-1937. Designed specifically for War Office service the Army began to take delivery of first orders in 1933. By the start of the war in 1939 both the Army and Air Ministry had some BSA V Twins listed as first line war machines. Recently information has come to light that many went to France with the BEF, and were later abandoned during the evacuation from the French coast. (IWM HU93235 & IWM HU93236)

MEE record the lightened version of the BSA War Office 498cc V Twin in 1935 after requests to BSA to reduce weight to improve handling. BSA made several changes including fitting a lighter saddle, lighter flywheels, gearbox casing, smaller capacity fuel tank and losing the rear pannier frame. The top of the frame was modified with weight reducing airship style 'cut-outs' but the final result was only 22lb lighter than the standard bike. The test of this one-off machine resulted in MEE deciding to search for a replacement for the V Twin altogether rather than continue with modifications on the test bike. (IWM HU93237 & IWM HU93238)

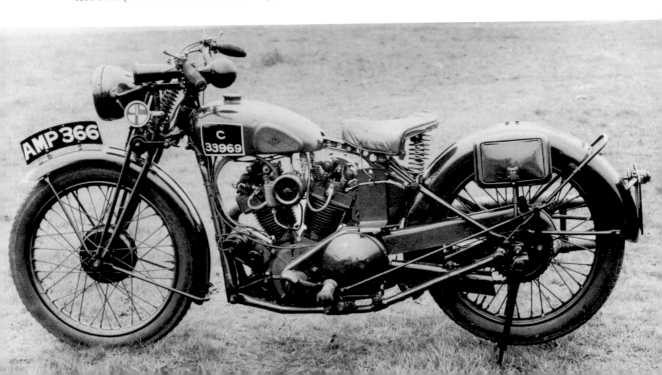

Left and right views of Royal Enfield's Model WD/D 248cc SV Single-Cylinder under test at MEE's Farnborough Depot. This was the first Royal Enfield model to be ordered in large numbers from the RE range of bikes with 600 requested in May, 1939. Via the Ministry of Supply they headed to the out-stations of the Department of Air Defence, employed in light communications roles. Essentially a militarised civilian Model D, even numbers of civilian Ds were pressed into Army service in 1940 for training duty, and female ATS riders. Model D production ceased in early 1941 and was not resumed for the duration. (IWM HU93248 & IWM HU71248)

Norton 16H prototype with experimental exhaust pipe fitted in efforts to reduce noise. (IWM HU93247)

Component testing also continued on the bikes that were submitted to MEE. Here an early experiment in moving the air cleaner of a 1936 Norton 16H 500cc Single-Cylinder machine to the right of the rear wheel is captured on film, designed to provide a mounting less likely to clog in desert or dry, dusty climates. Note a speedometer is not fitted. (IWM HU93246)

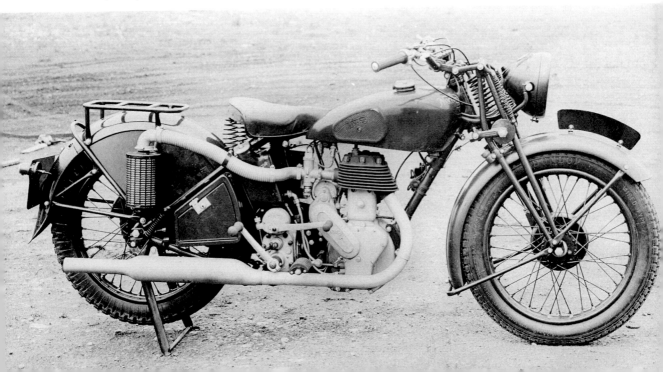

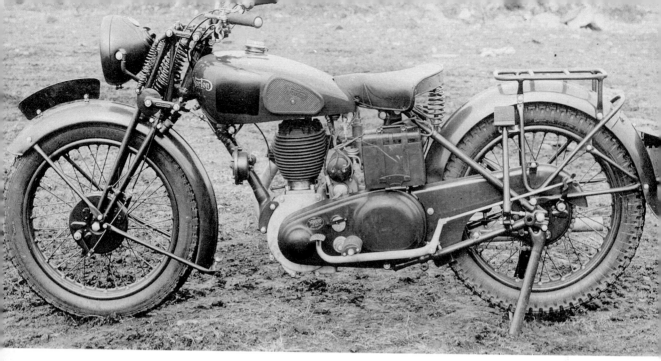

Another early Norton 16H under test, this one a prototype for the 1938 Model WD Norton 16H. Although a background has been painted on the side of the tank a C census number has yet to be added. During early war years the 16H went through a number of modifications including having pillion equipment, crankcase shield, addition of speedometers fitted and the removal of number plates and mounting brackets completed at issue. (IWM HU93245)

The BSA B20 249cc SV Single Cylinder Model of 1937-38 (H-B20 & J-B20). Another civilian specification motorcycle bought by the War Office with initial plans to utilise it for learner training, backed by light communication duties if required. Bought untested by MEE as it was not intended for frontline duty. (IWM HU93239)

The New Imperial Model 40, when used in the 1935 MEE trials. This was a 350cc OHV Single Cylinder model supplied in civilian colours, but at 7,000 miles into the testing process it failed to complete the rigorous tasks set before it due to engine wear and mechanical failures. New Imperials did make it into military service in small numbers at the beginning of the war but the company was never awarded a lucrative large contract. The motorcycles were designed using 'unit construction' which speeded manufacturing, and was not adopted as a sound manufacturing process by the British Motorcycle industry until the 1960s. (IWM HU93241)

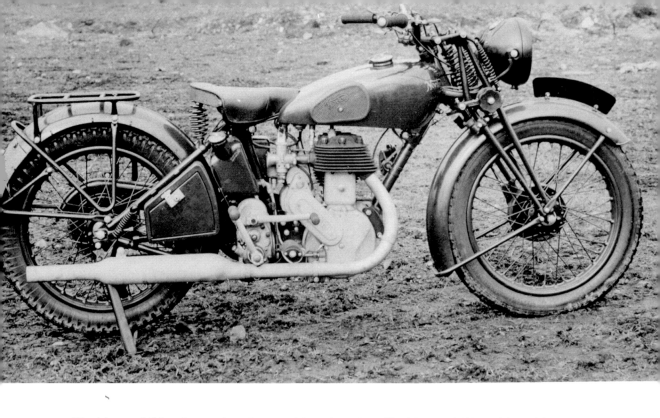

The Norton 16H under test in various model configurations. The Norton 16H model would prove to be one of the most widely used British motorcycles of the Second World War in every theatre. (IWM HU93244 & HU93240)

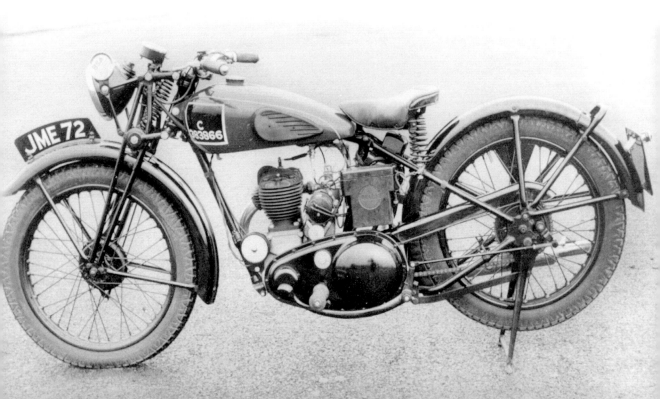

MEE shots of a 1935 Norton 16H on the day of its use in the 1935 trials. Tested in civilian paint trim, with pre-war registration displayed on number plates, the 16H proved to be the best 500cc motorcycle available that year and passed with flying colours despite noted mechanical failure in several areas including the headlamp bracket. The test process included fitting new handlebars and upgrading the engine sprocket with an extra tooth. (IWM HU93243 & IWM HU93242)

Motorcycle & Sidecar Combination Testing

Before the Second World War many manufacturers made their own sidecars to accompany the range of bikes available, however toward September 1939 and in the years following many made subsidiary deals with subcontracted smaller firms to maintain production levels with demand. Box bodies and a number of styles of sidecar were ordered to attach to a full range of bikes from the American Indian 741B to the BSA M20 and Norton 16H. A number of other sidecar developments were experimented with including a Mortar fitted sidecar for the Norton Big Four, and many variants of AA and ground use machine gun mounts for Lewis Gun to Bren Gun.

During the 1920s this service-intended sidecar combo was manufactured by Triumph. Illustrated here is the Model N 494cc Combination with weatherproof cover erected for sidecar passenger. By the mid-1930s MEE was looking to return to testing new combination designs. (IWM HU93253)

An early test of the 633cc Norton 'Big 4' (model No. 1) SV Single Cylinder SWD Combination with sidecar suitable for carrying a .303 armed Bren Gunner. In early tests the crew capacity was improved so three soldiers could travel with the addition of a pillion. With a driven wheel on the sidecar, cross country ability was viewed as excellent and by late 1938 it had passed all tests. Many were to see action with the BEF in France but the arrival of lend-lease Willys and Ford 4x4 Jeeps in spring of 1942 saw them ruled obsolete. (IWM HU82349)

When released on the surplus market after WW2 the Norton Big 4 had the drive to the sidecar wheel chopped out of the hub. The drive was originally designed through pre-war trials' experience by D.K. Mansell, the seat reminiscent of pre-war open top motoring! (IWM HU82347)

Deadly armament revealed, neatly stowed alongside the body of the sidecar is the butt of an early .303 Bren Gun. The axle to the driven sidecar wheel can be noted as can the addition of a folding windshield. (IWM HU82348)

The Northumberland Fusiliers return to the UK after action in France, amid claims of being the first British troops to cross into Belgium. Their motto 'Quo Fata Vocant' (Where the fates call) was foremost in their thoughts while training in fast reconnaissance exercises at Blandford Camp in Dorset during early 1941. Here motorcycle combinations of the 1st Bn park up in open space. The folding windshield has now been replaced by a handrail for the passenger. (IWM H3705)

1st Bn, Northumberland Fusiliers continue the exercise by moving off in strictly spaced columns during manoeuvres in Dorset during 1941. Unavoidable clouds of dust are raised as they move off. (IWM H3714)

During exercises in Northern Ireland on 15 April 1942 troops of the North Staffordshire regiment form the spearhead of an attack in mobile patrols of motorcycle combinations. Here these scouts take a section of covered road, armed with .303 Lee Enfield Rifle and Thompson .45 calibre SMG with foregrip. (IWM H18855)

In the South Eastern Command zone of the UK in 1941 it is the job of a mobile section of military policemen to put up road signs to direct troop movement. Here a party of MPs with Norton motorcycle and sidecars are ready to go out to erect signs. The signs, tools and lamps are carried in their utility box sidecars. (IWM H12814)

Summer 1941 – the .303 Bren Gun is weaponry demonstrated with Britain's motorcycle army – note how bipod is clamped around the handrail by rider. (IWM H13187)

These Northamptonshire men demonstrate how their motorcycle combinations can operate in a fast moving reconnaissance role in Summer 1941. (IWM H13181)

4th Battalion, Northamptonshire Regiment on exercise using combinations in a reconnaissance role at Omagh in County Tyrone during February 1942. Both are armed with .303 SMLE Lee Enfields and wear goggles of differing design. (IWM H17114)

29 August 1942 – a Norton Motorcycle combination is photographed as part of an airborne forces' request for shots of equipment in use. The leather padded bucket seat is reminiscent of pre-war motoring days. (IWM H23377)

19 April 1942, photographed by Lieutenant O'Brien of the AFPU, this shot of motorcycles and sidecars was taken in the Northern Command zone, UK, It features men of 27th Lancers who are backed up by a Mk1 Daimler 'Dingo' Scout car. (IWM H18870)

The Northumberland Fusiliers training as a fast mobile reconnaissance unit take a motorcycle and sidecar through a short cut which involves crossing ditches during an exercise in 1942 at Blandford Camp in Dorset. (IWM H3687)

A Norton combination is manhandled in demonstration photographs over rough chalky terrain and sandbagged obstacles in December 1940. (IWM H3683)

Troops in the Scottish Command zone start out on a day's exercise with .303 calibre Bren Guns at the ready on motorcycle combinations in December 1940. (IWM H5979)

Reconnaissance teams of the 4th Bn,
Northumberland Fusiliers. (IWM H3698)

Northumberland Fusiliers on exercise around Blandford Camp bump up onto level ground during a reconnaissance test set for new motorcycle combinations in the field in the summer of 1941. (IWM H3688)

'Mounted – and ready for action!' Norton combinations with 'cutaway' bodies to facilitate easy exit/entry to the sidecar. (IWM H3708)

20 March 1940 – on exercise in France the 4th Bn Northumberland Fusiliers are seen drawn up ready for the day's manoeuvres described as a 50th Division specialist unit for motorcycle reconnaissance operations. The Divisional double red T on black sign has been applied to the front shield of the sidecar. (IWM F3195)

Two British Tommies receive a welcome drink from a local Belgian girl – photographed by Messrs Ottnam, Kessell and Malandine on 10 May 1940. These were the scenes as the British army go to the aid of Dutch and Belgian forces at Herseaux. The 50th TT divisional sign is again applied to the sidecar. (IWM F.4342)

Chapter Three

The British Bikes

At the outbreak of war, two British motorcycling weeklies of the day, *THE MOTOR CYCLE* and *MOTORCYCLING*, printed campaigns designed to attract civilian motorcycle riders to the Royal Corps of Signals along the lines that, life in the forces on two wheels would be the apex for enthusiasts! The articles included registration forms which the enthused biker could cut out and complete in order to gain one of the *limited but coveted* places as a Despatch Rider. A letter had to be supplied with the returned form with 'full details of motorcycling experience, knowledge of running repairs, and list of machines ridden solo'. A medical grading of 1 had to be acquired also to gain entry, and those applying must be over twenty years old. Minimum height was five foot. For many pre-war bikers, this was the path of entry into World War Two. As the early years of the war passed, the entry requirements became less strict and with manpower shortages occurring in 1943, the Army was wondering whether it would ever find the numbers of men required for victory. The machines to be ridden nevertheless, were being received in large numbers, despite setbacks as factories in the Midlands were heavily bombed during the Blitz. The reality of 'army biking' was less glamorous at times. Alfred Francis Freeman, Royal Corps of Signals was posted to Headquarters, 7th Guards Brigade in 1939. A short time later he found himself in action in France. His role was to manage the Despatch Rider service for HQ.

> 'As well as allocating frequencies for the radios of Corps the DRLS (Despatch Rider Letter Service) was my main duty. This was later changed to SDS (Signal Despatch Service) but I would design the runs, work out how many times a day they would run, how many riders on which bikes – we had about 30 bikes at our disposal. The riders would set off round the various units within the Corps like the gunners and deliver what we called 'packets' – this was all the paperwork required to run the Corps – ration orders, administrative communication, letters from home, movement orders.'

John Collins served with 2nd Corps Signals, Royal Corps of Signals, also in the first year of the war. By Spring of 1940 he found himself riding his motorcycle in the fast moving fighting that was taking place toward the coastal towns of France after

German forces had pushed the British back toward Dunkirk. The valued DRs gained new respect for the prompt delivery of secret signals traffic in the field during this first experience of contact with the new mechanised German army. 'When operating in wireless silence in 1940 we saw the DRs come into their own.' Once at the beaches Collins recalled the chaos while troops waited for evacuation. There appeared to be very little organisation, and the exposed troops waiting in the dunes and in long lines wading out to the water's edge were in need of information. 'Being motorcyclists we got down to the beach very quickly, and then used our DRs to travel back and forth calling up troops to leave on the available boats.'

The evacuation at Dunkirk and other ports along the French coast has been portrayed as a heroic rescue, and it was, yet it also dealt a severe blow toward Britain's arsenal of vehicles and equipment. Urgent requests went out to high street motorcycle dealerships and training centres all across the land shortly after the return of the BEF for any machines that could be impressed into service with British Forces. For while large proportions of the BEF had been safely returned to the UK, a vast amount of their equipment lay burnt out in the coastal lanes and on the beaches of Northern France. By late 1940 motorcyclists and their machines were also being urgently sought by Civil Defence organisations in case of invasion, and ex-civilian impressed machines, often very rusty, were being issued to new riders, the majority of them women, who were learning about motorcycling for the first time. Training for the voluntary organisations was on an 'ad-hoc' basis in comparison with the army's training programme. One CD veteran recalled that 'my trainer said sit on the bike, switch on the engine, kickstart, then turn the throttle slowly. That all went OK but he didn't tell me how to stop! Luckily the bike stalled, after an extended tour of the local streets'. The military training received by those enlisted in the army often began with a tour of the controls of a BSA 350cc bike or similar. Once the purpose of clutch, throttle, brakes, etc had been explained the new recruits were often immediately instructed to ride the bike around the parade ground familiarising themselves with the controls. The first test was always whether or not the recruit could remember how to stop the machine, and there was more than one nervous rider who opened the throttle instead of applying the brakes only to roar off to a distant corner of the camp! Histon (Stan) Boreland had travelled from Gayle in St Mary, Jamaica after seeing advertisements that the 'Mother Country Needs You' in 1944. At just 18 years of age Histon completed eight weeks' basic training and then a motorcycling course at Weeton, near Blackpool. By 1944 the motorcycling training had been formulated into a succinct and successful course. Histon passed the course and spent the rest of his war years travelling between sister units of No 8 Bomber Group (Pathfinders) delivering and transporting packets/despatches in the Little Staughton area along the peaceful setting of English rural roads and tracks.

The British motorcycle industry had found itself ill-prepared for the outbreak of war despite the long rounds of trials and testing that had taken place since the mid-1920s. Constantly attempting to meet the changing requests from the War Office it worked hard to perfect a complex 500cc V Twin machine through the 1930s only to find the WO settling on the ideal configuration for an army bike of much more simplified design. V Twin engines were overlooked in the end for straightforward thumping singles which could be bulk built, and repaired much more easily. These machines were to be supported by a wider selection of smaller engined machines of the 350 and 250cc size and specialist machines or 'ultralightweights' would be used for specialised work. A new military specification was issued in 1938 but by the outbreak of war many of the manufacturers looking for military contracts were only just reaching prototype stages with newly designed machines. 3 September 1939 sounded alarm bells in Ministry of Supply depots and offices across the nation. The services would be short of the required transport they needed, and therefore to provide an instant remedy many civilian models were impounded, or impressed, from factories and showrooms across the country and this is demonstrated by the range of machines exhibited in the photographs of the following chapter – many still wearing civilian registration numbers and paint schemes and were over sprayed in khaki as time allowed but this task was hardly a priority under the threat of invasion. By mid-war the manufacturers caught up with demand, and REME depots were established to rebuild damaged machines in order to re-circulate machines already issued back into service. These bikes were often stripped to frame and rebuilt using all new parts thus few original wartime bikes exist today with matching frame and engine numbers for the collector. A large sample of survivors have various parts originating from different wartime contracts bolted to the same frame, and this is also due to the continued post-war service of many of these machines. BSA M20s and the Matchless G3 types continued long into the mid 1950s used as training machines and on active service. The following shots depict the British use of the motorcycle from the outbreak of war, through VIP inspections, to utilisation in combat theatres from Normandy to the Far East.

Prime Minister Winston Spencer Churchill inspects defences at North Coates aerodrome near Grimsby on 7th August 1940. These motorcycle combinations are first line defence should an airborne invasion launch. (IWM H2823)

On 16 August 1940 Mr Anthony Eden, Secretary of State for War inspects training areas in Southern Command. Here motorcyclists of the 7th Royal Warwickshire Regiment parade with their mix of machines, some with blackout light covers on headlamps, some still in civilian paint schemes on Worthy Down, Sussex. Camouflaged buildings in the background attest to the expectation of imminent German invasion, and these men carry gas masks and wear shoulder brassards which would change colour in the event of gas being used. Eden wears a brave face. (IWM H3162)

Here signallers attached to 5 Corps Southern Command demonstrate the deployment of the carrier pigeon carried in baskets in the event of radio communication being disabled during the expected German invasion of 1940. The white bar painted above the 41 indicated 'Corps' Troops. (IWM H3049 & IWM H3050)

Seated on Royal Enfield 346cc SV Single-Cylinder WD/C models, these troops are being given map reading instruction as part of their new role in 'Traffic Control' within Aldershot Command, hence the TC armbands and helmet stencilling. 6th August 1940. (IWM H2741)

9 April 1941, taken by Lt Malindine. Grenadier Guards become 'Tommy gun Motorcyclists' as part of mechanisation experimentation. These men of 1st Bn, Grenadier Guards of 7th Guards Brigade in 5 Corps test out new tommy-gun mounts fitted to their motorcycles. The experiments took place in Swanage but were not adopted for wartime use. (IWM H8826)

Another view of the 'Tommy-Gun Motorcyclists'. (IWM H8825)

9 July 1942 training session captured on film. Military Police riders allotted to armoured units learn specialist riding skills to work with tank formations. They are specifically trained in rapid front line movements assisting tank crews in finding off road cover, and also need to be expert marksmen and capable of providing small arms' firepower with a number of weapons. This warm July day provides perfect climate for musketry training in the butts with the .303 SMLE Lee Enfield and the American Thompson .45 calibre sub machine gun. They wear a mix of boots with gaiters and the newly designed despatch rider's buckle boots. (IWM H21879 & H21880)

29 July 1942. The Provost Marshall Major General Sir Percy Laurie, KCVO, CBE, DSO inspects another RAC attached MP unit in the Newmarket area. These men and their machines originated from the 9th Armoured Division training in the area. (Note Panda Divisional recognition sign painted on the front mudguards, a tongue in cheek crack at 'Panzer' Divisions of the German forces.) (IWM H21903)

During the 9th Armoured exercises in and around the Newmarket area during 1942 the movement of Covenanter Tanks is regulated and guided by the Traffic Control riders. Here a rider has authenticated the route using his own map and waves on the armoured column to its next way point. (IWM H21903)

At 36 VRD (Vehicle Reserve Depot) hundreds of motorcycles are stored in the outbuildings of a disused brickworks somewhere in the UK. These bikes are yet to receive divisional or regimental markings, but are fitted with blackout headlamp covers and the left row have tyre pressure (TP) guidance stencilled on their front mudguards. Vehicles in storage were continually maintained in a state of readiness. An ATS girl can be seen checking the cabling on BSA W-B30s. (IWM H37319)

Equipped with saddlebags and pillion seats these BSA WB-30 bikes are inspected prior to issue in another building which comprised 36 VRD (Vehicle Reserve Depot). (IWM H37317)

Royal Enfields are lined up in storage with standard wartime blackout headlamp covers fitted to their headlights. (IWM H37318)

At an RASC Depot in Feltham girls of the ATS inspect civilian painted Army commandeered motorcycles which have received their 'C' census numbers but are yet to be stood against a wall and given the once over with the olive paint. (IWM H570)

This shot was taken during the winter of 1939 on the Sussex Downs and describes the London Irish Rifles involved in motorcycle training. (IWM H1203)

Photographed by Captain Console, Army Film and Photographic Unit, the original caption reads 'The second BEF leaves for France: Scots, Canadians and Yorkshiremen embark with their motorcycles as the Band of the Royal Marines played them off from Southampton Docks – 15 June 1940'. (IWM H1792)

Patrolling the coastline at home these Army motorcyclists roar across the Sussex Downs on the search for German parachutists – 12 August 1940. To adhere to the blackout the headlamp glass on each bike has been painted over. (IWM H2980)

On 16 August 1940 the South Wales Borderers exercise on the suburban streets of Bootle near Liverpool in a planned anti-invasion exercise. These men are described as 'a motorcyclists fighting column' and ride equipped with sidecars, and singles, all wear gas detection brassards and carry the .303 SMLE model rifle. (IWM H3095)

A shining pre-war Model 40 New Imperial bike and Essex LDV rider (one of 2000 Local Defence Volunteers on parade) presented to HM The King in 1940. With traditional oily rag tucked behind the seat, it is otherwise spotless and retains a civilian front number plate. It is likely to be the rider's own pre-war mount although small numbers of New Imperials did find their way to the War Office when Triumph took over the company and a few were built up from remaining spare parts at their old Coventry factory before new model production took place. 20 July 1940. (IWM H2372)

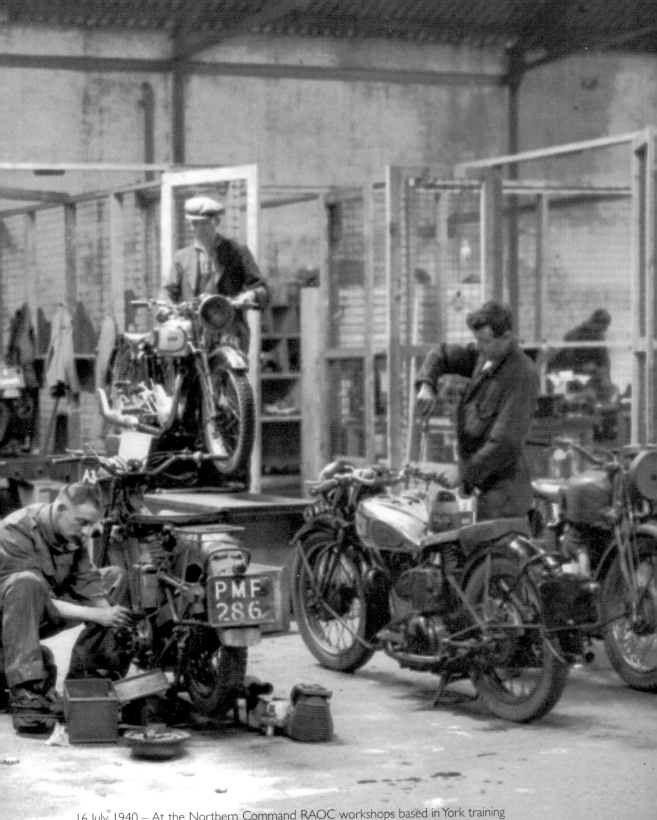

16 July 1940 – At the Northern Command RAOC workshops based in York training continues with an MT Class being taught motorcycle maintenance while civilian employees continue to service machines. A range of civilian and military paint schemes are present, as are the civilian number plates of bikes impressed into service. (IWM H2281)

1940 – An instructor crests a hill on a 1938 Rudge Service Model, possibly one of the handful of test models provided to MEE. Twelve were bought under contract for further testing between 1938-39 and another order for 200 of these machines was made although it has been thought until recently that they were all destroyed in an air raid. The instructor here belongs to an unidentified London based T.A. Signals Unit and also rode as part of a T.A. motorcycle display team. (IWM H1522)

Photograph taken during exercises by 405 AA Battery, RWAFF. A mechanic from the WAASC Maintenance section rebuilds an engine having replaced the valves on this bike and readies it for continued service with West African Forces in May of 1942.
(IWM WA 84)

A despatch rider hauled across a river aided by a squadron of Royal Engineers who put on the demonstration to illustrate how everything from a Bren Gun carrier to a despatch rider and his motorcycle could be ferried across rivers by using assault boats lashed together or individually at Tanfield training area, Yorkshire. Units involved were 53rd (W.Y.) anti-tank RA, and 16th Field Squadron, Royal Engineers in 1942. (IWM H20585.)

On campaign in Normandy. Major Taylor (right) Commanding Officer of 10 Field Hygiene Section, 12 Corps instructs Sgt Howarth to use his motorcycle to take the daily work detail out to dispersed units. 10 Field Hygiene Section were operating with 24 Casualty Clearing Station of 12 Corps during this busy period – 12 July 1944. (IWM B7020)

Motorcycle maintenance classes continued throughout the war on the home front at RASC driving and maintenance schools. (IWM R37390)

C-in-C General Alexander visits British workshops in Gura before personally flying himself on to Khartoum. Here he examines a Matchless G3 model with rear wheel accelerating to maximum revs while the bike is secured on a workshop bench. The Matchless logo (winged 'M') can be seen on the side of the tank. (IWM E21074)

In the Middle East – a new mobile library service to entertain the troops has been provided. Here three men originating from Leeds man the lonely station, they are left to right Cpl L Manningwell, L/Cpl Cooper and Trooper Ryan. This motorcycle delivered selected reading materials. (IWM E29705)

12 July 1944 – having received instructions from their officer, NCOs of the 10th Field Hygiene Section, 12 Corps set off on a tour of their areas of responsibility in Normandy on Matchless G3Ls. They would orchestrate the burning of old ration tins to kill all germs, to finding fresh water supply. The motorcycle was the fastest way to cover the ground. (IWM B7021)

Pte Bertha Ball, aged 21, hailing from Derby and a pre-war worker at the Rolls-Royce factory now works as an ATS fitter in a motorcycle section of a REME workshop, here receiving instruction on the assembly of army Norton 16H motorcycles after just seven months' service. (IWM H24366)

Army BSA riders line up for a publicity shot to demonstrate how they can quickly produce weaponry to challenge an enemy from the saddle. They are armed with a range of versions of the American .45 calibre Thompson sub machine gun. (IWM H5989)

2 & 3 October 1941 – Lt General Carr, Army commander in charge of 'Nazi Invaders' during a Bumper invasion exercise toward the close of 1941 is provided protection as he travels the battlefield by motorcycle outriders. (IWM H14416)

Chapter Four

The American Bikes

Due to the amount of WWI surplus machines still in circulation during the 1920s and 1930s the US Government required very few new machines from manufacturers who had survived the depression in the States. In North America the survivors were few and far between, just Harley-Davidson and Indian. In 1932 the first fresh order for Model R Harley-Davidsons was made – just 100, then a year later a further order filtered through of 312 VDS models fitted with LT Sidecars, plus only 9 RL solo models. Further odd orders came through but the first mention of a potential War Department order was not mooted until 1937 with a selection of Model WLs. The WL model had a been a mainstay product for the civilian solo rider throughout the 1930s with 750cc engine and the larger U and UL Models with 1200cc motors. Fifty were requested, and two years later in 1939, the National Guard were presented with forty-six Model Ws. Indian, the only other major US manufacturer vying for military contracts, were surviving on supplying the nation's Police forces countrywide but both companies were holding their breath for the lucrative contracts to supply the military. Indian had led the way with Flatheads (side-valve engines) and their range for military consideration included the 750cc Model 640, which later evolved into the 500cc Model 741B Scout and the larger Indian 340B Chief of 1200cc capacity. The smaller bikes were disliked by the military although they were appreciated by the US Navy and US Marine Corps (USMC) who took delivery of a few. Some of the early production Indians were sent both to Britain and to France under the lend-lease scheme, and equipped Czech and Polish armies in the UK and fared well as exports however there were problems with the models which created hesitation for large scale ordering at home.

This decision threw the spotlight back onto Harley-Davidson who were considering which of their civilian models might be quickly militarised. In August of 1939 HD despatched a pair of side-valve militarised WL models (designated WL-A for Army) off to Fort Knox in Kentucky and to the QM Depot at Holabird where the prototypes of the Jeep would be tested six months later. The Army began a tough process of testing which saw the WLA model adopted after design changes. The Harley-Davidson WLA (named The Liberator by the people of Holland in 1944) appeared to be the bike most favoured by US troops for any future war. 89,000 WLA models would be manufactured during the war by HD at a cost then of between $370 and $395 each. The US Army took delivery of 60,000 although other orders of bikes went to Britain, Russia, Australia and even China. Variants were built only for the Canadian National Defense (CND) and were designated as the WLC model and were delivered from August of 1941. The first orders from the US Army came in during January of 1940 just four months after the testing had taken place at Holabird and Fort Knox. At first 421 WLAs were asked for then 5,000 just a few months later. The WLA was in production continuously until August 1945. That first WL model to receive the Army's procurement test differed from production model bikes (WLA 1942) in

Wartime Cushman scooter advertisement – scooters parachute into action with twin canopies

several respects. Fitted with elongated 'Buckhorn' handlebars, larger diameter wheels, and 3 inch longer forks it also retained its civilian speedometer, early pattern lights and featured a high mounted headlamp above the handlebars. Even after adoption of the WLA the Army tested other models made by Indian, and even as late as 1943 were considering the Indian 841B of which only 1000 were made.

Both manufacturers had experienced a good relationship with the military during the First World War, although Indian had gone all out to secure wartime contracts from 1916 while HD preferred to keep their civilian buyers and dealer networks happy while supplying the Army in much smaller numbers. In WW2 Harley-Davidson also responded to the War Department's request by producing a machine very similar to a pre-war BMW R71 design and called it the XA, (Experimental Army type). It has often been suggested that the XA was a nut and bolt copy of the BMW R71, however this is unfair as it was only the cylinder barrels and some gaskets which were interchangeable. What did interest the Army was the elimination of chain drive replaced by shaft drive. Chains had always been a problem with motorcycles, especially in a military context requiring continual adjustment or time consuming replacement. On the XA model, both primary drive and dynamo drive were via gears. Indian chose to build a bike from scratch. The Indian 841B (Model no 8 of 1941 – with Battery) was Indian's first effort at a foot change machine, and its first and last design to feature a shaft drive. It utilised hydraulically dampened forks, rear springs, front and rear interchangeable wheels and centre stand to park the bike upon. However, by the time the manufacturing run of the first 1000 841Bs were produced the wartime Jeep made by Ford and Willys-Overland had won the military vote. Further orders were cancelled in favour of more jeeps. Although the motorcycle was much more mobile than many of the components of other motorised units, the more traditional motorcyclists' tasks were being taken over by four wheeled vehicles towards the middle and end of the war. Sidecars became totally outmoded although the solo rider remained as convoy escort and messenger carrier to war's end in 1945. The Indian survived into post-war years of course and thanks to much of the wartime innovation engineered by its designers their post-war models featured rubber mounted shock proof handlebars, new forks and much better brake design. Harley-Davidsons are found today in every city on the planet! This is how the American machines looked throughout the last war.

Cushman 244cc airborne scooter here in use by the US Navy – built in Lincoln, Nebraska with the same intention as for the British used Welbike. The Cushman scooter it was hoped would help airborne forces with provision of disposable immediate transport on landing in occupied territory. The bike used a cylindrical fuel tank and was powered by a single-cylinder four stroke engine of an industrial design. Its simple frame design included parachute mountings to facilitate delivery to the battlefield without the use of a protective container. Here wounded German prisoners rest on stretchers at the quayside in a North African port. They are guarded by USN and Army personnel, and will soon be transported to more permanent POW enclosures. (IWM NYP19597)

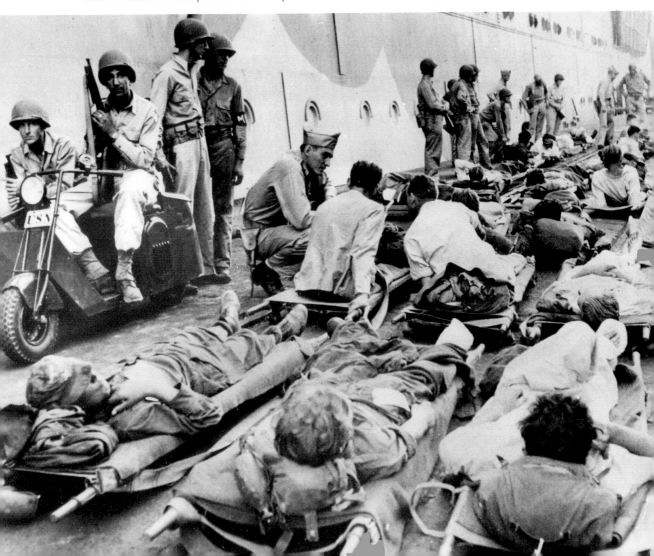

Training covered by US Press photographers in Kentucky during exercises by a US armoured brigade. These riders appear to be equipped with early war model (1939) 750cc Harley-Davidson WLs and ride out in front to plan the route for the armoured column of Stuart tanks following them. Note the headlight position mounted high above the handlebars on these early models compared with later models featured in this chapter. The riders wear HBT tank coveralls, with the Tankers' jacket over the top. Goggles are worn on cloth helmets for training. (IWM AP11279B)

At a US camp training in Australia this rider tore into position at 35 mph, laid the bike down in a controlled stop, and was in action with his .45 acp Thompson SMG in a further three seconds – the wartime caption exclaims. A good view of the leather saddlebags and double rear light cluster is provided. (IWM HU78870.)

Pristine troops in training wheel a Harley Davidson WLA model from an aircraft mock-up during training in the US in 1942. This shot provides a good view of the cavalry inspired leatherwork which included a rifle scabbard for the .30-06 MI Garand rifle and the saddlebags fitted over the rear mudguard. (IWM OEM1294)

20 May 1944 – Pvt Wilburn L. Cummings, Military Police, of Carmi, Illinois jumps his 750cc Harley out of a shell-hole while on training manoeuvres in Britain. Leg shields, headlight casing, and front of the mudguard have been painted white in accordance with both blackout regulations and to distinguish MP motorcycles at a distance from other military motorcycles using the roads. (IWM EA20452)

American Military Police on Harley-Davidson WLAs training in the UK – note the crossed flintlock pistol logo of the US Military Police on the windshield of the bike nearest camera. Rear view mirrors, leg shields, and mudguards have been painted white as well as the windshields to help visibility in Britain's blackout. (IWM EA22451)

Sgt John M. Shelley of Greensburg, Kentucky was one of those on the exercise, riding HD WLA number 17. The wartime censor has obliterated specific unit markings on the front mudguard (20 May 1944). (IWM EA22449)

The US military police riders were expected to be as competent off road as on road with their machines and practise traversing shell-pocked battlefields on this section of the commandeered British countryside. (IWM EA22450)

20 October, 1943 – a youngster too small to either reach footrests or handlebars in Palermo is treated to candy and a taster of motorcycling the American way. The rider's goggles have been tucked over the horn, and a vehicle air raid siren has been fitted bottom right to the front forks. (IWM NY3565)

A clear view of the simple construction of the rifle scabbard bracket attached to the front forks of a Harley Davidson WLA at this allied message station during exercises. Field telephone and typewriter convert orders for the smartly attired despatch rider to deliver. The enlisted man's tie was discarded in combat theatres. (IWM NYT51087)

During the invasion of France in 1944 a unit of American Military Policemen ride en masse through the outskirts of Cherbourg soon after the city had been taken in order to restore law and order, and impose some regulation of traffic flow. (IWM PL29583)

Salvage depots sprang up all over the European Theatre of Operations to keep the fleets of military vehicles in operational condition during the advance to Berlin. Here Sgt Charles Anton of Seattle, Washington (right) and T/4 Robert Pipkin of Kinston, North Carolina work on a stripped down frame. Harleys and Indians litter the workshop which is why Sgt Anton earned the nickname 'Champion Junkman of the ETO'. (IWM AP173)

In the centre square of the French village of Percy an M10 tank destroyer follows a Stuart reconnaissance tank through a motorcycle traffic control post on 2 August 1944. (IWM EA32289)

A Canadian WLC model Harley-Davidson in service in North Africa at a sandbag protected wireless message centre. A pilot receives instruction as a DR brings in paper signals to be sent out over the air waves. (IWM CM1329)

US Military Police motorcyclists serving in Britain providing traditional aid through the unfamiliar streets of London in convoy escort role. The column of GMC 6 x 6s may have spent hours motoring around without their help. Two of the outriders in front of the first truck are named as PFC Rossa West and Pvt J. Zuideme. (IWM HU60571)

'Snowdrops' of a Traffic Control Section of the US Army Military Police are photographed on their Harley Davidson WLA motorcycles on active service in Britain. They are fitted with a variety of blackout covers and the fifth bike from the front wears a stars and stripes flag across the windshield. (IWM HU57512)

US Military Police motorcyclists stop traffic at a crossroads in London on 21 March 1944. They wear British issue steel despatch riders' helmets, but American Mackinaw ('jeep coats') and standard M41 issue US uniforms other than this. They are Pvt Jacob Zuideme of Kalamazoo, Michigan and PFC Foster of Duncan, Jersey City. (IWM HU60568)

Corporal A. Power, a member of the Canadian Provost Corps, checks the driving license and work ticket belonging to a military vehicle driver on 11 January 1943. He rides a shaft driven Indian. Both the chrome bumper of the staff car and mudguard of his bike have been painted white to increase visibility in the British blackout. (IWM HU56801)

This Indian was commandeered by the ENSA organisation and was used by the proud rider Captain Bert Ellison formerly of the RASC to organise the tours of recently liberated territory and to find theatrical venues where troops could be provided entertainment. Anna Neagle and Rex Harrison were two among so many of the ENSA entertainers who were already famous, or who would be, in the post-war years. (IWM HU73320)

A US Despatch Rider awaits answers for his superiors at a 113th Provost Coy RMP Information Centre set up at Bayeux railway station. The American rider wears the tankers' helmet of US Armoured Forces, and his motorcycle is equipped with Thompson SMG in a leather scabbard and binoculars fastened in their case between the handlebars and headlight. (IWM B6458)

Harley-Davidson motorcycles, typewriters and wireless sets taken by French Forces in North Africa and then recaptured. The factory applied USA registration number can be seen applied to the bottom of the rear mudguard below the light cluster. (IWM E31020)

An unidentified Canadian rider entertains local children during an exercise with Britain's Home Army on a Harley-Davidson WLC.
(IWM H28023)

The Royal Air Force move into action on Harley WLCs during the Normandy campaign on the ground too as TAF (Tactical Air Force) convoy outriders await orders to move nearer to Creully where fierce fighting was taking place to clear the village, west of Caen in June 1944. The TAF ground units would liaise with Typhoon aircraft already airborne and co-ordinate attacks in support of Allied ground forces. (IWM CL774)

British Officers in Rome who love the Harley-Davidson! (L to R) Captain T.W.M. Greenhill of London, Captain W.L. Wilson, Lieutenant Mackenzie of Edinburgh. They are all from the Allied Military Government section in Rome and administer the occupation police. Many were pre-war policemen and detectives. The front mudguard is clearly stencilled AMG – POLICE. (IWM NA16303)

16 May 1941. With invasion still on the mind, Polish troops in Perthshire, UK play the role of defending against British troops playing Germans in another invasion exercise. This tommy gun equipped Indian motorcycle combination is typically camouflaged in an early war scheme. (IWM H9779)

Polish forces in Scotland check over their equipment during routine maintenance. Here a 1200cc Indian 340B motorcycle combination has its sidecar separated from the bike. The camouflage pattern on the sidecar incorporates a map of Poland, and home towns marked upon it by homesick Poles. (IWM H21265)

Canadian volunteer troops enjoy tea and biscuits from a NAAFI wagon during a reconnaissance exercise in 1940. The Indian combination has been fitted with a .303 Lewis Gun on an anti-aircraft mount. It points skyward behind the standing trooper in the sidecar. A mix of First and Second World War issue kit is present as is the early DR helmet clearly based on pre-war racing designs. (IWM HU53511)

Other Indian combinations pull up to the NAAFI wagon moments later, this time equipped with .303 Bren Guns. The rider on the left wears the standard infantry helmet along with goggles. The later steel rimless DR helmet allowed the wearing of goggles which could be easily positioned above the rider's face when he chose not to wear them, 1940. (IWM HU53513)

Chapter Five

The German Bikes

In 1938-39 the German Army were using a number of mainly civilian designed motorcycles taken into service. An example of this type was the NSU 201 ZDB 'Light Motorcycle' which was powered by a single cylinder two-stroke engine of 200cc. It produced 7hp and had a four speed, hand changer gearbox running on slim 3.00 x 19 tyres. Along with the lighter bikes were a number of heavier bike-sidecar combinations which steadily took over in production. The NSU 201 ZDB was only produced for about a year and yet NSU were soon to be engaged in producing one of the most unusual motorcycle projects of the 39-45 war –

Kleines Kettenkraftrad Type HK 101, Sd.Kfz.2 – 'The Kettenkrad'

Originating from German pre-war experimentation the motorcycle hybrid known more commonly as 'the Kettenkrad' proved a popular vehicle on all fronts from North Africa to Russia with German Forces. It was a concept that came from the mind of Heinrich Ernst Kniepkamp in June of 1939, and the concept was developed further in trials by the NSU Motorenwerk company culminating in a production model of this small tracked motorcycle. Variants of the Kettenkrad were produced from 1940 throughout the war and continued until 1948. At first viewing, it does look like a motorcycle of sorts, but its purpose was intended to fulfil personnel and ammunition transportation rather than the despatch carrying and recce roles assigned to the heavy bike-sidecar combinations. Its first trials proved it to be a successful line layer, and so early production models (Sd.Kfz.2/1 & Sd.Kfz. 2/2) were fitted with brackets to hold telephone wire wound on drums. It could pull a small two wheeled trailer, and even towed the smaller anti-tank guns, often being used in difficult terrain to re-supply troops with ammunition and rations. Therefore it is probably most closely related to the allied Bren Carrier types in its actual intended field use. The Kettenkrad had excellent off-road ability, a range of 150 miles on one tank, climbing a 1-in-1 sloped terrain, with a wading ability of 18 inches in depth. The rider operated it from a rather exposed position however, and was seated between two fuel tanks! Rider comfort came in the form of a large padded pan saddle, and cushioning rubber pads were fitted to the interior of the bulkhead to protect his knees when traversing rough terrain. He was also able to provide transport for two passengers who sat at the rear of the vehicle on a rearward facing bench seat, their weapons stowed in vertical rifle racking, but close to hand. Officers needing to inspect front line positions would often jump aboard for a bumpy if assured tour of their forward defences.

However, study of the photographs of Kettenkrads in this chapter also suggest some of the problems encountered in this design when it was utilised in the arduous conditions of modern warfare, and there were plenty. It was un-armoured and unarmed for starters making it and its riders vulnerable to small arms' fire in frontline positions. The front forks were the weakest part in the vehicle's construction. On paved roads it did ride well, but the whole assembly was weakened by excessive cross-country use and would fracture, breaking away from the rest of the bodywork. The remedy for this was at first to strengthen the original spoked wheel, with a hardier solid version as seen in this chapter, and very soon removal of the wheel completely was the instruction given to riders when taking their vehicles cross-country for long periods. The wheel of course was not required for steering, as the track mechanisms worked as they did in tanks, braked left and right by a turn of the handlebars. This instruction even featured in later captured riders' manuals. At the same time NSU were working on producing a sturdier front fork arrangement and investigating losing the front handlebar arrangement altogether. There was also the question of training riders to operate the Kettenkrad which required most skill cross country. Smaller turns could be made by using the conventional handlebars and the 19 inch diameter front wheel. Simply after applying the turn, a linkage would engage which connected to the front drive sprockets of the tracks. This applied differential braking common to wartime tracked vehicles. With some skill and variation of the turning of the handlebars the rider was thus able to control the turning radius. With one track totally locked up he was able to squeeze out a 12 foot turning circle, but with a high centre of gravity and across uneven terrain this sort of manoeuvre was hair-raising at the very least! On tarmac it was also incredibly loud, clattering along and certainly could not be used in a stealthy environment on the battlefield. The Kettenkrad with crew of three weighed one and a quarter tons, and could travel on tarmac at speeds up to 40mph powered by its Opel 1500cc water cooled engine. The engine had originated from the pre-war Opel Olympia saloon car, but was now mounted centrally in the Sd.Kfz. 2/1 & 2/2. A few of these remarkable machines survived the war into museum captivity and private ownership and they are always guaranteed to provide an interested crowd when fired up at the many restored military vehicle shows which take place around the world!

German forces were also famous for their use of bike sidecar combinations.

In 1935 BMW began work on their R12 model. Intended as a touring design for the civilian market it featured for the first time on any bike telescopic front forks with hydraulic damping. The German motorcycle industry had long been prepared for the outbreak of worldwide conflict lead by innovation created in the world of motor sport. BMW, DKW and NSU competed in the 500cc racing class in the late 1930s, and in the smaller 250cc DKW dominated. Underlying these sporting successes was the propaganda pushing the image of Germany as world leader. On the home front in Germany large numbers of smaller motorcycles were being produced and made available to the public and thus in return the nation was gaining a populace experienced at both riding and maintaining these machines. In 1938 further preparations were stepped up with the rationalisation of manufacturing industries. The multiple motorcycle types and variants on offer numbered somewhere in the region of 150 and these were reduced to just 30 types; the array of engines on offer were standardised so that just a few were offered to power these thirty models. Many manufacturers had the type of motorcycle they would produce enforced upon them, but parts production saw the greatest reduction in surplus labour effort and over-complication. Items such as saddles, number plate stamping plants, and electric horns were reduced to a single design type of which chosen companies were allowed to produce. The process was successful, simplifying the stores management, the re-supply of parts quickly, and allowing saved funding to be redirected into the war effort elsewhere.

Like all the participants of the Second World War, the German army's views towards two-wheeled warfare also covered several trends. Commencing the war with a vast majority of solo machines, from two-stroke torobust flat twins paired with sidecars a change of preference occurred after 1940. A move then leant toward the complex and expensive BMW and Zundapp combinations in the mid-war period but with industry pressed by the Allied bombing campaigns production of these machines was phased out through 1944 and Germany returned to production of 125cc and 350cc machines in the last year of the war, DKW being the sole German manufacturer to continue motorcycle production between 1939-1945. The following images depict the broad range of machines in use with the German Army in WW2.

By June of 1940 it was clear that there would be no stopping the German advance through the countryside of France. The spearheads of armed motorcycle combinations, followed closely by infantry and armoured support had forged through to the coastline. The Phoney War was over. An Iron Cross wearing NCO motorcyclist harasses an elderly French woman as other motorcyclists await orders to move further forward on the Pont sur Seine. (IWM HU93297)

Caked with dust, two riders share cigarettes by their Zundapp K800W motorcycle after delivering urgent messages on the eastern front in 1941. This official German photograph originates from the propaganda series 'Das Heer Im Grossdeutschen Freiheitskampf' (The Army in Great Germany's Struggle For Liberation). (IWM COL161)

A DR with full combat load packed onto his Zundapp DB200W bike. Visible are gas mask container, water bottle, bed roll, bulging saddlebags and a leather briefcase on the fuel tank. France, 1940. (IWM HU93289)

Despatch motorcyclists dig out their Zundapp K800W motorcycle and sidecar combination which has bogged down in the mud of the Eastern front in Spring 1942. The sidecar is fitted with typical canvas tonneau cover, and the spindle for mounting spare wheel to sidecar is also visible. (IWM COL167)

20 May 1940 – as motorcycle infantrymen advance through the outer suburbs of Amiens others stop for a short rest. This German DR wears goggles atop his helmet and standard issue long rubberised coat. His face is blackened from the spring dust thrown up in the advance through France, and his bike heavily stowed with tools, stores, spares, and personal baggage. (IWM HU93289)

A 35(t) tank and motorcycles pursue the enemy through Spring dust in France, 1940. The sidecar combination nearest the camera appears to be a BMW R12 flat twin with telescopic front forks. (IWM HU93283)

An abandoned 250cc NSU with Afrika Korps pith helmet attached to the front forks. The remains of the engine oil and fuel leak into the sandy puddles left by a desert rainstorm. (IWM E19359)

Convoy rests in the town square market place of Ravilly in France on 19 June 1940. Note waterproofed canvas tonneau cover for side-car passenger, the only member of the three man crew provided any protection other than clothing. (IWM HU93290)

On the Aisne Canal, 10 June 1940, the narrow pathways and steep tracks along the south of the canal were perfect ambush points. A combination is wrecked alongside other bikes near a felled tree. Other dumped trucks can be seen abandoned on the tree line. Resting on the fallen tree trunk is the rider's helmet, replete with bullet hole through its crown. (IWM HU93286)

A familiar sight on the cobbled streets of occupied towns – the constant flow of military traffic would often contain several BMW or Zundapp 750cc combinations. The sidecar in the rear carries an additional spare tyre over the front bodywork. Both motorcycles in this instance appear to be KS600Ws. (IWM HU70696)

BMW R12 Flat Twin combinations pulled up in Prague outside the gates of Hradany Castle in the Reich's Protectorate of Bohemia and Moravia, now the modern day capital of the Czech Republic. (IWM HU75736)

The three man standard
Wehrmacht motorcycle
combination crew
demonstrated, with
sidecar armed with the
rapid firing MG34 machine
gun. Leg shields, and
sidecar design are unusual
but front forks resemble
NSU Kettenkrad design.
(IWM HU46942)

11 November 1942 – a
motorcyclist is given a baby to hold
while surrounded by Bulgarian
women in National Costume
during this 'spontaneous' outpouring
of happiness as the German Army
enters Bulgaria. (IWM HU3165)

Various unserviceable
single bikes are dumped in
a ditch as the advance to
the French coastline
gathers momentum.
Sturdy BMW R75
combinations roar by as
an onlooker inspects the
wrecks for spares.
(IWM HU93288)

German motorcyclists triumphantly collect a captured Russian airman and prepare to transport him to a fate unknown on their BMW R12.
(IWM HU93288)

Waffen SS motorcyclists push a combination through the long Russian summer grass. Note the SS license plate on the rear mudguard of the bike. (IWM HU93285)

Captured German motorcycles appeared to create a source of interest and excitement amongst British troops – here a 350cc DKW is photographed within a collection of photographs which covered entry into Germany. (IWM HU93293)

Close-up of the captured 350cc DKW engine fittings – including the centrifugal air cleaner. (IWM HU93292)

15 December 1941. British troops learn to ride a German BMW R75 combination during a respite from the fighting around Tobruk. Note the detail of the Afrika Korps palm tree/swastika emblem. (IWM E7089A)

Dead Afrika Korps motorcyclist by his machine at Mersa Matruh in November 1942. (IWM E19317)

Many captured motorcycles along with a range of weaponry were put to good short-term Allied use in the front line. This photo was taken by Sgt Mapham, AFPU on 15 June 1944 and shows British Glider troops showing off a captured German Zundapp 2 Stroke to a local French girl. The glider men are from Kent, London, and Surrey and are now armed with British and German small arms. These men came in with gliders which landed at 12.20am on 6 June 1944. (IWM B5585)

A Turkish cadet sits proudly on his German manufactured 250cc NSU – note the NSU logo prominently displayed on the tank. (IWM K1738)

Finnish Campaign – skis were used experimentally to propel motorcycle combinations in a variety of designs and adaptations, and similar designs were adopted by Axis and Allied forces where conditions of deep snow prevailed. (IWM HU74711)

Kettenkrad – The Tracked Motorcycle

November 1942, North Africa, and this Royal Tank Corps officer takes some men for a spin in a captured Kettenkrad and trailer. The front mudguard has been removed which became an operational instruction soon after their issue which facilitated easy changing of damaged front wheels. (IWM E12940)

Sgt Gunn (AFPU) photographed this captured NSU Kettenkrad on 23 July 1943 during the North African campaign. A Notek blackout light is fitted to the front mudguard but headlight has been removed from the front fork bracket. (IWM NA4920)

A close up view of the captured Kettenkrad featured in IWM E12940. (IWM E12942)

A fire damaged Kettenkrad which was towing two 2cm Flak guns photographed abandoned on 3 May 1945 in Lubeck, Germany. This Kettenkrad has been fitted with a solid disc front wheel. (IWM BU5195)

The Italian designed Vologrufo airborne parascooter used by the Luftwaffe, and captured by British troops as they entered Rome on 6/7 June 1944. (IWM NA16100)

6/7 June 1944. The double front wheels of the Volugrufo are demonstrated in this shot as a British serviceman tests out the scooter on the streets of Rome. (IWM NA16101)

At war's end came the return to transport of times past. Isolated groups of Germany's defeated army continued to surrender, in this instance to the US Seventh Army. Unescorted, this malnourished horse-drawn convoy, stretching back into Austria carries soldiers and their wives and girlfriends into captivity – 22 May, 1945. (IWM SFC45)

Chapter Six

Specials, Races, Motorcycle Displays

Desert racers and Scratch-built machines produce racing clubs like the 'Bar None'

How to keep soldiers occupied outside of daily duties has always been the task of those in command and with the desert war and liberation complete in the North African Middle Eastern theatres Brigadier J. Chrystall CBE MC and Brigadier H. J. Hayman-Joyce originated one solution for motorcycle riders of the armed forces in the region. Forming the 'Bar None' MCC, so-called Championship Trials were held in Cairo and surrounding areas over a rocky terrain segment and dusty flat desert course. Machines were taken from local service breakers' yards and stripped down or modified in base workshops, and the event grew in size due to keen membership and the desire of spectators who would travel from across Egypt to experience the thrills and spills. The club flourished and continued on return of the many members to the UK. Other groups formed display teams, as are demonstrated in this chapter at the Vienna military tattoo of 1945. Display teams provided not only a demonstration of motorcycling skill but an entertainment with a 'hearts and minds' approach toward the local populace. The traditional military motorcycle display team exists to the present day of course. Elsewhere on the Home Army front other cross-country trials and road-races had been organised throughout the war to engender competition, excellence and release from the pressures of participating in total warfare. Pre-war TT racers and stars of speedway often organised or fronted these events, taking the opportunities to pass on tips and advice to the service riders. The following images record some of these events proving the service life of the motorcyclists was not solely about getting the message through.

Racing on local roads in the UK – Sgt J.H. 'Crasher' White and legendary Freddie Frith (TT winner and pre-war works rider for Velocette) retain manufacturer loyalty and rode Velocettes throughout 1942 while training new riders. Crasher's machine has had the headlight removed to lighten road weight. (IWM H24685)

Reminiscent of 'Tourist Trophy' days Sgts Crasher White and Freddie Frith give a speedy demo of fast cornering on 29 October 1942 during a training demonstration at the RASC Driving School, Lake District, Cumbria. (IWM H24689)

Another shot of Sgt J.H. 'Crasher' White and legendary Freddie Frith (TT winner and works rider for Velocette) while training new riders. (IWM H24690)

Corporal Cady Cox provides helpful advice to new riders taking part in a cross-country motorcycle trial. Cox was Southampton Speedway team captain before the war.
(IWM HU93311)

Lance Sergeant R. Bainbridge in leather jerkin, DR breeches and double buckle high boots, recently joined a DR company and will be responsible for training 'riding style and technique' exclaims the wartime caption. Bainbridge was a well-known trials' rider pre-war.
(IWM HU93312)

Captain Graham Oates, RASC, on his BSA, was the wartime organiser of many trials and demonstration days for new motorcyclists. Oates was also a pre-war 'name' in British motorcycling circles.
(IWM HU93313)

Lt Col R.C. Atwill of the RASC, described as a great champion of motorcycling within the British Army, and a frequent contributor to 'Motorcycling' magazine.
(IWM HU93314)

The Ultimate 'Special'?

Perhaps the ultimate 'special' machine constructed during the war – Tech/Sergeant Edwin Kikovski, American of New York, riding his own invention – a special scooter constructed entirely from scrap aircraft parts he was able to scavenge around the airfield at Bari in Italy during 1944. Kikovski would proudly ride his machine around for visiting aircraft. (IWM HU33292)

Display Teams and Racing

In 1940 this TA Signals Unit originating from London practise manoeuvres on modified pre-war civilian Rudge Trials bikes including jumping over burning hay bales using wooden ramps! (IWM H1527)

The same TA Signallers utilise a range of bikes in everyday use and for their displays from the Rudge Service Model of 1938 on the far left, trials' models from pre-war years centre, to the BSA far right. (IWM H1518)

Signals DRs train for a display at the Vienna Military Tattoo of 1945 – described by the original caption writer as a 'difficult balancing feat' on this Matchless G3L machine one is inclined to agree!

One can see the original caption writer found some light relief in these annotations – again rehearsals for the Vienna Military Tattoo take place. Signalman Mackenzie of 1 Holm Quarry Road, Kilmarnock is described as placing 'lots of trust' in Signalman G.E. Moffatt of Wakefield, Yorkshire. Mackenzie is jumping over Moffatt's bike being ridden at some speed. Other tricks these signallers rehearsed were '12 men on a bike' and 'fire jumping.' (IWM VIE1460)

DRs train for the Vienna Military Tattoo. After a day's riding has been completed for display team rehearsals the mechanics set to work servicing the bikes. Signalman J. Henderson, also a fitter, of 10 Sulerwells Crescent, Lancs (left) and Signalman L. Cooper of Third Avenue, York attend to oil leaks. (IWM VIE1466)

24 March 1941 – motorcycle trials took place in Ripon, Northern Command Zone with a hundred officers and men. Mr A. Jeffreys, a well-known civilian pre-war motorcycle demonstrator, toured the command area and gave advice to the Army riders during the trials. Competitors are seen here struggling with their machines up a steep hillside which formed the final obstacle. (IWM H8414)

The Middle East Motorcycle Trials – 21 May 1945. Thrills galore were to be viewed in the shadow of the Pyramids in an all service Open Hill Climb. 100 competitors with winner emerging named Craftsman Plain, of No. 5 Sub Workshops, REME on a Matchless. One of the highlights of the meet was a challenge match between Brigadier H.J. Hayman-Joyce, Cairo Area Commander and patron of the 'Bar None' Motorcycle Club and Air-Commodore J. Oliver, RAF. Here they are on the start line! (IWM E30968)

Craftsman Plain of 213 Whitchurch Road, Cardiff on the right, and Sergeant R. Oaks of 28 Fox Hollies Road, Huddersfield who won first and second place awards for their efforts in the hill climb. They also scooped the cup for the winning team, and awards for the fastest ascents in the sand. Both display their trophies on their modified Matchless machines. (IWM E30969)

Sgt Mapham of the AFPU – using a captured Italian bike, Mapham and his AFPU 'Circus' used the bike to take exposed films back to Head Quarters. Mapham wears improvised headwear which appears to be an early AFV Tank Crew helmet, and smokes regardless of the likelihood of fuel leaks! Mapham's photographs covered both the desert and NW European campaigns. (IWM E20130)

2 June 1945, 6th South African Armoured Division hold a motorcycle reliability trial at Arcole, 10 miles northeast of Milan, Italy. The trial was held over ground used for pre-war civilian motorcycle testing and Mr Gilera, manufacturer of well-known Italian motorcycles, gave the silver cup for best individual performance. Here WO J.W. Sauerman riding a BSA foots hard to gain the top of a bank after clearing a deep mud puddle. (IWM NA25476)

The Bar None Motorcycle Reliability Trials

27 February 1945 – the Bar None Motorcycle reliability trials in Cairo – more than 1500 spectators saw Sgt Syd Hufton, Royal Signals roar to victory over a stiff desert course in the shadow of the Pyramids. Leading Aircraftsman Baber of the RAF has difficulty negotiating a section comprised only of loose sand. (IWM E30680)

The members of the winning team, Bar None Trials in Cairo: (L to R) Sgt W.D. Stopforth of 4 Greens Cottage, Aigburth Vale in Liverpool, Sgt S.J. Hufton of 45 Sampson Road, Birmingham and Lance Corporal McAdie of Welling in Kent. (IWM E30685)

10 February 1945 – a 100 competitors took part in the Palestine Army Motorcycle Trials at Latrun, Palestine. Ten hazards were set out on the course calling for considerable riding skill. A competitor tackles 'Bechers Brook' at speed and manages to pass through without any loss of points. (IWM E30611)

This shot was taken split seconds before a competitor came to grief on his Matchless machine over an observed section of the course on the Palestine course in 1945. (IWM E30612.)

14 August 1942 – and a 'Busman's Holiday' captured on film. Members of 59th Recce Regt (original caption) at Markethill, Co. Armagh in Northern Ireland join in a motorcycle trial 'just for recreational fun'. An incredible leap is captured off a dirt earthwork ramp bolstered by logs, across a water-filled pit. (IWM H22472)

Training in 1942 – steep hill climbs form part of basic motorcycling proficiency where the army is concerned. (IWM H21498)

December 1941 – motorcyclists are trained on a trials course by riding between flags and under barriers on a more basic instructional course. (IWM H16088)

British Designs
for Airborne Motorcycles

Not strictly 'specials' the British designs for airborne-dropped motorcycles do deserve separate focus. The Welbike as illustrated over the next pages has already been discussed in the introduction to the book but its partner was the 125cc Royal Enfield Flying Flea. Both lightweight motorcycles were adapted for use by Airborne Forces from a design idea that harboured very different intentions. The James ML and RE 'Flea' were very similar model designs based upon the pre-war German DKW RT100. The James was equipped with a Villiers 122cc engine and three speed gearbox. It also featured folding handlebars and became fondly known as the 'Clockwork Mouse'. Around 6,000 were manufactured during the war. The Royal Enfield 'Flying Flea' was powered by a 125cc engine, about 8,000 were produced, and it even came with a specially designed dropping frame made from tubular steel to protect it during descent via parachute. All three machines feature in the following images.

9 June 1943 – British Airborne troops retrieve a delivery of Welbikes from equipment containers at Bulford Camp in a posed photograph – note absence of any parachute canopy attached to container. (IWM H30628)

Welbikes found their way to many theatres of operation. Here one is used by RAF personnel in North Africa as an airfield runabout in 1943. (IWM CM6866)

An official shot of a Mk I Welbike, serial number C4659218, taken for the record by MWEE at Farnborough in unfolded configuration. (IWM KID5361)

An official shot of a Mk I Welbike, taken for the record by MWEE at Farnborough to record handlebars and saddle retracted in the folded position ready for loading into an equipment container. (IWM KID5359)

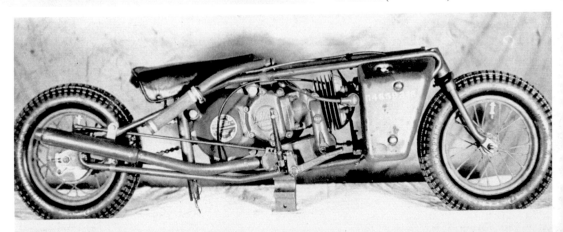

Although new equipment for Airborne Forces was a closely guarded wartime secret the battle to convince Press and public opinion that troops were being provided the very best kit to accomplish the job never ended throughout the war. One such display of Airborne equipment was photographed here in Birmingham although it was unlikely that these photographs made it into the newspapers before major combat operations were to take place. (IWM D19288)

More Welbikes photographed as airfield runabouts in North Africa. Note the machine on the right has had a new serial number repainted vertically down the length of the fuel tank 'WD 90367'. (IWM CM6665)

9 June 1943 – with petrol consumption averaging 180 miles to the gallon these Parachutists are eager to lift their new Welbikes carefully over wire fences during manoeuvres at Bulford Camp, UK.
(IWM H30631)

Two paratroopers reach speeds of 40 – 45mph on 9 June 1943 during the same demonstration at Bulford.
(IWM H30630)

A Polish airborne
unit is captured on
film using Welbikes
in pre-invasion
exercises.
(IWM MH1147 & 1148)

The Welbike was started by running them along and letting the clutch in – two paras start their engines. (IWM H30629)

Removing the Welbike from its container on the battlefield is demonstrated during yet another exercise. (IWM H30627)

A demonstration takes place of the Mk2 Welbike, this time fitted with rear mudguard helping to avoid mudsplash to the rear of the rider. (IWM MH11486)

MWEE demonstrate a range of mechanical devices which could be delivered to Airborne Forces on the battlefield via air-dropped equipment containers. At the front is the Welbike secure in folded-down configuration within a container, Jarrow tractor can also be seen. (IWM MVE11152/2)

1943 – another press demonstration of secret airborne equipment takes place in the build up to the invasion. (IWM H27481)

5 February 1943 Welbike exercise held at Bulford camp. This shot depicts 'the folding Welbike and its container'. On the lid of the container carrying the Welbike can be seen the words Motor Cycle in 2 inch lettering. This is the CLE Mk I canister. (IWM H27061)

Despite the many rehearsal exercises for air-dropping the folding motorcycle before the Normandy Invasion, Welbikes were also carried ashore fully assembled on 6 by several units. (IWM B5217)

6 June 1944 – British 2nd Army, RM Commandos of Headquarters, 4th Special Service Brigade make their way from LCIs onto 'Nan' Beach, at St Aubin-sur-Mer at about 9am carrying assembled Welbikes. Identified in the photo are E. Hall, W. Sendal and H. Douglas. (IWM B5218)

Taken by Lt Spender of AFPU these shots depict men of the 1st Airborne Division displaying their new Welbike design on 29th August 1943; note the large dent to the fuel tank. This is one of the six black painted prototypes, note the unpainted flywheel. (IWM H23384)

Another of Lt Spender's AFPU shots depicts the 1st Airborne Division displaying their new Welbike design on 29th August 1943, again a probable original one of the six prototypes. (IWM H23384)

3 February 1943, specialist airborne forces equipment is put on display for a press day at the Royal Ordnance Depot, Greenford in Middlesex. On show with the Welbike are Denison camouflaged smocks, equipment baskets and containers, and folding parachutists' bicycles. (IWM H26963)

5 February 1943 – another Welbike demonstration is provided. The D-shaped nature of one half of the specially designed drop containers is clearly demonstrated in this photograph. (IWM H27060)

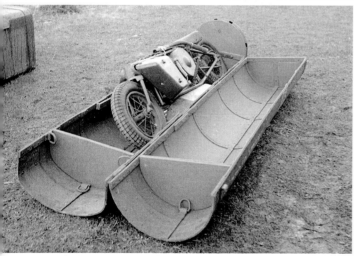

Welbike C5152421 is photographed in the role it played most frequently during the war in most instances – the convenient and disposable 98cc runaround. Like most of his kit, the Welbike was probably scrounged en route. (IWM CLA3576)

The 125cc Royal Enfield Flying Flea
for Airborne Forces

A British Airborne modified Jeep (modified to reduce weight for glider transportation) and a 125cc Flying Flea airborne motorcycle are demonstrated in front of the Airspeed Horsa Glider which delivered them to Normandy and later Arnhem and over the Rhine, 22 April 1944. (IWM H37694)

22 April 1944 – a paratrooper lifts a 125cc Flying Flea to demonstrate the lightweight design during an Airborne forces demonstration day. (IWM H37691)

Specially designed dropping cages of tubular steel were invented to protect the lightweight 125cc airborne motorcycles during their descent to the battlefield. (IWM MH37216)

The specially designed dropping cage of tubular steel invented to protect the lightweight 125cc airborne motorcycles during their descent to the battlefield is seen here with parachute pack attached. The motorcycle is ready to be thrown out of an aircraft at 800ft! (IWM MH36036)

On 6 June 1944 Royal Marine Commandos head inland with equipment and pushing a James 'Clockwork Mouse' to conserve fuel for use only in running communications' errands. The small machines were often believed to have only been parachuted into battle for use by Airborne troops but were known to have been sent in by glider, and carried ashore in the coastal assaults by ship. (IWM B5220)

Chapter Seven

The Wartime Motorcyclist's Uniform

I refrained from calling this chapter 'The Wartime <u>DESPATCH RIDER'S</u> Uniform' as officially it was only the Royal Corps of Signals who had the right to call their motorcyclists Despatch Riders. The other arms were to officially call their riders 'Motorcycle Orderlies' although the abbreviation MO never caught on amongst the troops when referring to the motorcyclists within their own units. The wartime motorcyclists enjoyed the reputation of being a law-unto-themselves, and were clearly identified by their separately designed uniforms from other vehicle mounted troops. This chapter considers some of the weatherproofing and protective clothing issued to British wartime motorcyclists, and it was the British and Canadian forces who received most specialised uniform and equipment for motorcycling. In writing this chapter I am reminded of an ex-Don R I met at a museum one afternoon. He retold an account of a 'DR initiation' ceremony for the new entries who were marched over to the hut where the jack-the-lad motorcyclists' section in his RAF Signals unit would loiter on the camp. At the time this group were specially designated to deliver 'Sealed Orders' by hand, and by hand only. A potential recruit to the section would be tested out by being offered a simple spin on the pillion. Unknown to the keen new face the old lags would have a specially prepared uniform wardrobe and equipment which facilitated this *audition* process. Boots were provided a size or two too small, with specially prepared prickly insoles, and then once seated behind the rider, the recruit was kindly instructed to place his hands around the instructor. Instantly his hands were handcuffed and boots clipped to the pillion foot-pegs before the bike roared away into the night with said recruit screaming for dear life. (They had neglected to inform said recruit their instructor was a TT race champ.) If he survived the initiation ceremony, he was then welcomed warmly into the 'in-crowd'.

The uniforms both accepted into service and experimented with in this chapter clearly intended to protect the rider, whether from weather or premature dismount. Often based on pre-war racing or trials wear, the kit worn by the British Motorcyclist in the Second World War became one of the most recognisable uniforms worn in all theatres of the 39-45 war. Weather protection was dealt with by the Rubber-

Proofed Coat, Pattern 1942: constructed with a tail that could be brought up through the crutch and buttoned up over the rider's stomach, also fastening around each leg with strong brass press studs. The coat was issued from c. March 1942 onwards, and was introduced to replace a variety of waterproofed leggings, jackets and coveralls which had all proved to be unsuitable after testing through the first years of the war. Motorcyclists like to 'mix and match' issued kit and this is clearly visible from many of the photographs which appear in this book. DR Cord Breeches are often worn with BD Blouse and the ubiquitous leather jerkin. The breeches were of the pre-war 'Mounted Pattern' and were similar to the designs worn by general officers during the First World War with reinforced seats. Also known as 'Pantaloons' they began to be issued from July 1941 to other ranks who were to receive motorcycle training. They were only to be worn on duty and were not intended to replace the standard battledress trousers issued to all. The Leather Jerkin originated in the First World War proving a comfortable and hard wearing garment which saw widespread use in the trenches. Manufactured out of dark brown hide leather, with a khaki blanket lining it also provided warmth when riding. With no collar or sleeves, and fastened closed by four front buttons it was ideal for the seated riding posture of the despatch rider. The jerkin was favoured amongst RASC drivers for these reasons, and became a trademark for Brigadier-General Brian Horrocks of XXX Corps during the campaign in Europe.

Army Council Instructions (ACI) were given in early 1942 regarding the wearing of crash or protective helmets while riding motorcycles on active service. In ACI 545 of 14 March 1942 attention was drawn to the maintenance of protective headwear as much as the wearing of it. It detailed the importance of wearing a helmet properly, inspecting it for damage, and the recognition by the rider that his or her life depended on this piece of equipment. While the American and German armies were happy to let their motorcyclists use standard infantry design helmets when operating as motorcyclists, the British army went through a number of design alterations before arriving at the famous Despatch Rider's Helmet, Mk I.

At the outbreak of war motorcyclists simply wore soft hats and goggles or the British infantry Mk I through Mk IV helmets, a recognisable development from the Brodie pattern First World War steel helmets. These were found to be unstable on the rider's head, and provided little protection in the event of a fall – the rim likely to scuff along the ground creating further injury by jerking at the chin strap under the rider's chin. There were some 'pulp helmets' issued, based on pre-war racing crash helmets and manufactured from a toughened papier-mâché mould. Proving far more successful, lightweight, rimless, and comfortable in comparison to the infantry helmet, further orders were placed. The pulp helmet became the standardised motorcyclists' helmet up to c July 1943. Produced in a glossy green initially, it was then produced in matt khaki, with orders from ACI after 1941 to paint all remaining gloss examples a matt shade. It sat higher on the rider's head than the later steel helmets due to its internal sling construction, part of which could be seen looped around the outer edge of the helmet and a feature which makes these Despatch Rider's Crash Helmets (First Pattern) or 'Pulp Helmets' easily recognisable in photographs. The helmet utilised a leather neck surround which also formed the chinstrap replacing the notion of a single sprung canvas chinstrap as used on the infantry helmets.

By July of 1943 a combination of accident study and wear and tear appraisal produced the realisation that a motorcyclist's helmet manufactured from steel was required. The Despatch Rider's Mark 1 Steel Helmet was the result. With its introduction came the phasing out of the earlier pulp style helmets. One helmet for each officer and other rank, and later to the ATS who were in possession of a motorcycle or sidecar, was agreed in ACIs. The accident study had revealed a high proportion of injuries suffered by motorcyclists on active service were head injuries and specifically fractures of the skull. Compulsory wearing of the DR steel helmet it was hoped would drastically reduce these figures. There were a few exceptions to this Army-wide instruction involving training purposes, or 'other circumstances' when advised to do so by War Office, C-in-Cs or GOs, C-in-C. The earlier pulp pattern was reduced to Home Guard issue and remained in local service until the end of the war.

Footwear was also designed specifically for the British Army motorcyclists and was available from July 1941. The boots designed were for wear by any other rank who was tasked with riding a motorcycle, but were only intended for wear during motorcycle duty as at all other occasions personnel were required to wear standard web anklets (gaiters) with ankle boots. Further changes to the motorcyclist's boot came in 1944 as the motorcycle industry made every attempt to conserve use of rubber and replace it with other materials. Canvas handlebar grips had been used in pace of rubber, and in 1944 footrests and kick-starters were deemed parts no longer to be encased in rubber on newly made machines. Therefore the metal plates that had been fitted into the middle of the right boot for protection were deleted, and those boots already manufactured had the plates removed and wooden plugs placed into the screw holes.

Gauntlets and goggles form the other specialised clothing lines aimed at the wartime British motorcyclist. Standard issue MT Goggles were being issued to drivers before the war as many of the 15cwt vehicles used aero-windscreens typical of the period. The goggles were issued in a cardbox, one per driver and featured cotton sprung backing to a pressed alloy frame, elasticised strap and plain glass lenses. Later in the war splinter-less glass was used. Additional to these came a mid-

Two months after the outbreak of war in November 1939 this motorcyclist with freshly painted Norton 16H, still bearing a civilian registration number and yet to comply with blackout regulations is photographed participating in an army transport demonstration at a small arms' school somewhere in the UK. Note he still wears items of Great War equipment including puttees, and leather water bottle carrier. He has yet to be issued with any specialist equipment other than his goggles which he wears around his neck. (IWM H446)

war issue of 'Eye-shields Anti-Dust and Anti-gas, Mark I' which were a closer fitting plastic flexible pair of eye-shields favoured by some motorcyclists, and these again were issued one per driver or rider. Many riders opted not to protect their eyes or scrounged goggles either locally manufactured or of patterns issued to other Armies. Leather gauntlets were another adopted protective clothing design, although mainly seen on ceremonial duties some DRs can be seen wearing them in forward frontline areas. Problems of keeping warm verses the inability to work quickly in dextrous tasks such as fastening buckles, making adjustments to the bikes while wearing them dissuaded many from wearing gauntlets on offer as issue clothing.

The following photographs illustrate much of this equipment in use.

Evacuated motorcyclists from the K.O.S.Bs from the BEF in France return with the mounts to Southampton Docks in May of 1940. Bikes and men were loaded on the M.V. Delius which made the crossing back to safety. Note how some of the riders use their Infantry style helmets as blackout covers over headlamps. One man at the rear of the group wears DR gauntlets but there is little else in the way of specialist equipment exhibited. Long woollen greatcoats mix with BDs.
(IWM H1841)

Post-Dunkirk testing took place for over a year on deciding appropriate equipment for the Army motorcyclist. This photograph captures final testing before standardisation of uniform on 6 August 1941. The man on the left wears an 'International Suit' made of weatherproof treated cotton twill and the man on the right wears DR double-buckle boots, rider's breeches and BD jacket. Both men wear early fibre helmets. (IWM HU93310.)

The weatherproof 'Coat Skirt' on test 6 August 1941. This garment came down well over the boot tops in the riding position, and was designed as the coat for the International Suit all-in-one rider's uniform. (IWM HU93306)

Wearing denim battledress tunic and trousers as working dress a fitter repairs this Norton 16H with fuel tank and head removed. Other than coveralls the denim working dress served perfectly for maintenance tasks. (IWM H7735)

Wet weather conditions such as these required specialised clothing design to keep riders dry. (IWM H5626)

Improvised wet weather gear, rubber Wellington boots, waterproof leggings and mackintosh protect this rider from mud. (IWM 5330)

17 September 1941 – Britain's motorcycle army on exercise at Friary Wood Farm, near Colchester in the Eastern Command Zone of the UK, taking time to test the newly issued waterproof equipment.
(IWM H13971 & H13970)

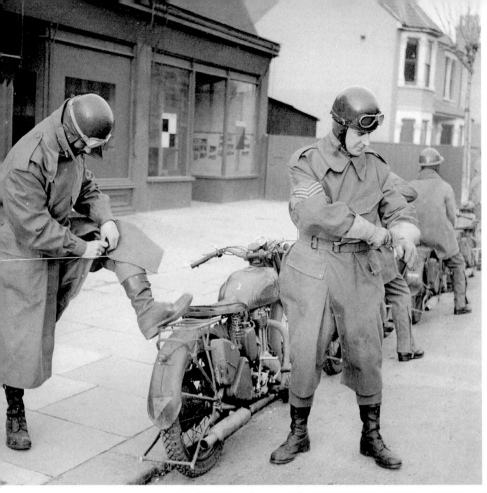

Part of the 6 August
uniform tests included
experimentation with the
rubberised overcoat and
motorcyclist's breeches.
(IWM H26531)

The Mackintosh
rubberised overcoat for
British Army
motorcyclists is unveiled
on 6 August 1941.
(IWM H26530)

The Zipp-fastener 'International Suit' under test in August 1941. This garment was based on the exact suit worn by Great Britain's pre-war racing team and underwent some heavy testing. It was eventually rejected for general issue in favour of the more versatile breeches and BD jacket combination. (IWM HU93309)

The Mackintosh was equipped with a range of stud fasteners at the wrist closures to ensure waterproof travel for the rider whatever his size. (IWM HU93308)

The wartime motorcyclist also required specialist footwear as the standard army boot provided no protection for shin or lower leg, and its sole was studded with hob-nails. A new boot was also standardised during the tests of August 1941 and is seen here on an early outing. Much higher than the standard boot, it fastened by lace and double-buckles providing protection to just below the knee. (IWM H26532)

December 1942 – a British rider is protected from the gathering rain clouds by rubberised leggings and a ³/₄ length rubberised mackintosh on the road in Tunisia, 1942. (IWM NA228.)

Home Guard motorcyclists not only had to provide their own machines to ride when on duty but were expected to provide their own protective equipment. This man, an American serving with the HG wears fisherman's waders and belted ³/₄ length leather coat. He wears a civilian helmet with full vision wraparound goggles strapped upon it. (IWM KY1686B)

In more temperate climates British motorcyclists opted for light cotton KD uniform, including shorts. A despatch rider of Royal West African Force in collarless KD work shirt. (IWM NA77)

14 November 1942 – RSM Atkinson of the Beirut Army Fire Brigade takes instructions before leading the fire engine on his motorcycle choosing the quickest route to where the fire is located. The force was made of entirely British troops, augmented by local Basutos. KD shorts may have been cool weather-wise but provided zero protection from a fall. (IWM E19522)